RESIDENT ON CALL

RESIDENT ON CALL

A Doctor's Reflections on His First Years at Mass General

SCOTT A. RIVKEES, MD

LYONS PRESS
Guilford, Connecticut

An imprint of Globe Pequot Press

Lyons Press is an imprint of Globe Pequot Press.

Project editor: Meredith Dias
Layout artist: Melissa Evarts

Library of Congress Cataloging-in-Publication Data

Rivkees, Scott A.
  Resident on call : a doctor's reflections on his first years at Mass General / Scott A. Rivkees.
    pages cm
  ISBN 978-0-7627-9453-9
1. Rivkees, Scott A. 2. Massachusetts General Hospital. 3. Residents (Medicine)—United States—Biography. 4. Residents (Medicine)—Training of—United States. I. Title. II. Title: Doctor's reflections on his first years at Mass General.
  R154.R445A3 2014
  610.92—dc23
  [B]

                                                                                    2013050234

Printed in the United States of America

10 9 8 7 6 5 4 3 2 1

These stories are based on real events. Some of these stories are described as they occurred; others are compilations of a series of real events; and others are what we imagined happened or hoped to occur. They have been modified to protect the identities and confidentiality of the individuals discussed.

This work is for Jack, Hans, Marco, Don, Steve, and Pete, who shaped my medical soul and are my eternal and special friends, even though some have passed. Most of all, this book is for the living and departed whose care was entrusted to me—a special privilege for which I am indebted—and for my family, Tina, Mike, and Ben, who tolerated a life in medicine that perpetually pulled me from home.

Contents

Introduction
Reflections on the Charles

I have been at Yale for fourteen years, a professor of pediatrics at the Yale School of Medicine. I am sitting at my fake wood–top desk on a gray fall Saturday as Hurricane Irene is about to hit New Haven. I am looking out my window at an ugly tan brick research building as the rain begins. I am just about to ink a letter of offer that will make me the chairman of pediatrics at a major university.

As I grip a blue pen, I look up from my desk at a picture that has always hung in front of where I sit. It is a faded color photograph taken at a special symposium held in honor of the retiring chief of pediatric endocrinology at Massachusetts General Hospital in Boston.

I look at that picture and see good friends, some dead, some retired, some still in Boston and at Harvard, but mostly I see friends who have moved on to other universities. I close my eyes and hear the voices and laughter. I hear their admonitions and encouragement. I look at these individuals—the souls who shaped me as a physician and person.

As I am about to sign this letter of offer with joy, I know it is not I who should be holding the pen but rather they. I am their surrogate, their trainee, who over eleven years—three as a resident, three as a fellow, and five as a young faculty member—soaked in decades of their collective wisdom, brilliance, kind nature, discovery, good humor, and friendship.

It is their soul in my hand more than mine. It is their song to me that says, "We have met our obligation to you. You now meet your obligation to the next generation."

While I think of the venerable individuals who trained me to become a physician, I think of my Boston soul mates, my fellow interns and residents in training who, like me, entered the demanding, electric, driving world of Boston and Harvard Medicine, where we struggled in earnest to become doctors. There we also struggled to cast our lives beyond the clean hospital walls. We fought the emotional exhaustion of providing complex care while brutally sleep deprived. We fought the despair following the death of our charges and encounters with child abuse. We struggled to set our identity and autonomy in a nondemocratic system of a medical apprenticeship.

And among all the wretched tribulations and stress, we found a way to see and make humor in it all. Perhaps this was because the amusement made the serious moments and tragedies fade, making our days of training, which would be otherwise unbearable, some of the greatest days of our lives.

This reflection is a memoir of the special days, the special circumstances, and the special people who made me and my young colleagues the physicians we are. Like all reflections that go back many years, some are fuzzy, some are bigger, and some are smaller than reality. Some reflections may be the outcomes and tales we were hoping for rather than what happened. Some reflections are of the grand stories told in a basement cafeteria as we huddled around plastic-top tables during our late evening meals, when we ducked out of the wards for twenty minutes of peer socialization. We chose to believe these stories were real, knowing they were perhaps not.

But these are my reflections from a special dimension in my mind, emblazoned during a special time of my life—along the Charles River in Boston at Massachusetts General Hospital, which we affectionately and mockingly called "Man's Greatest Hospital."

In this reflection, I first see myself as a young medical school graduate with an inferiority complex about having gone to a state school and now swimming against a sea of Harvard and Ivy League alumni. I see my good friend for life, "Wags," who entered Man's Greatest Hospital to train in surgery and who by chance I roomed with in a rodent-infested apartment, chasing companionship and dodging heartache during our precious time off. I see Fenway Park, the Cape, and the bars in town, our essence of sanity in an insane world of disease. I see how we pondered the difficult cases and navigated a way to learn among one-upping overachievers.

I see how we prevailed over the exhaustion, the mistakes, the deaths, and the threats of disease and persons. I see how the long days and nights of training stacked on top of one another, giving us needed confidence to care for precious lives and futures.

I see the occasional arrogance of youth—a consequence of our rapid promotion from student to doctor without having lived much in between—that could make us seem cavalier, cold, and uncaring. But this was unintentional and would be later reined in by wisdom and age.

As I reflect, I see there was no one time, neither after a tragic code nor after a case of meningitis cared for, that would make us step back and say, "Now, I'm a doctor." Our training never done, humbled by our perpetual inadequacy, we were made "doctor" only by the salutations of those who addressed us as such.

And in a flat reflection on the Charles River, I see the green beginning of my time in Boston—the compass for my career that started like the first arc swing of a pendulum clock, the timekeeper that started the first day I pulled onto Storrow Drive.

But the emptiness of the reflection of the day I drove out of Boston for the last time, more than a decade later, the day the pendulum stopped, lingers more. That was the day I took one last over-the-shoulder glance at a reflection on the Charles, wondering if the wink I saw in the ripples of the river was real. Or was it just a duck?

First Glimpse

We were the lucky ones, the chosen ones, the overachievers—all with the social delays wrought by too many years of schooling. We came to train at Man's Greatest Hospital, entering with fear and doubt and with often nervous, sometimes hopeful imagining of the days ahead that would in the end turn out to be far from reality.

I remember my first glimpse of the hospital where I would spend the next decade of my life. Visiting with friends in Boston the night before my interview for residency, following the S-curves of Storrow Drive on a rainy night, reflecting on the flat waters of the Charles River, I saw the redbrick facade bearing the black steel letters, not the granite I was expecting of Massachusetts General Hospital.

I was newly hatched from medical school in New Jersey, and this was where I and the others would learn to become doctors. This was a time we'd have no names, known only for our roles, our quirks, and our infamy. We'd be so immersed in work, so consumed by responsibility, that we couldn't tell you who was president, governor, or senator.

We came from different parts of the country and different colleges. Some were descendants of governors, senators, and presidents. Some were the sons and daughters of stockbrokers, car dealers, firefighters, and engineers. Some were the first in their family to graduate from college; others were on their way to becoming fourth-generation physicians. Those from the Ivies—Harvard, Yale, Princeton—might have had the edge on day one. But we soon saw that we were all the same—the same products of the same books, the same notes, and the same bland lectures. We were to be later distinguished by our drive, creativity, and judgment.

Twenty-four years old, and still buoyant from medical school graduation, I came to Boston with more trepidation than exhilaration. I was the son of an achieving businessman who would say, "Hard work is rewarded by harder work." My mother was a wildly compassionate person who would say, "No matter how much it costs, we'll spend the money to have your big ears pinned back."

When I arrived, they called me the "runner-up resident." In high school I finished a no-podium second in science class rank. Six feet tall and lanky, I finished second in the state section championships in the half mile. My college was my second choice—the state school, Rutgers, that took a backseat to Princeton. In college I again finished a no-speech just out of my class top. A collegiate rower, I was on a team that placed second to Harvard in the national championships.

My medical school in Newark was a second-tier state school. There I finished just out of top of my class. I played rugby on medical school weekends, and our team finished second to Columbia in the New York–area medical school rugby championships. My parents and friends said, "Second is still great!" as I again sighed.

My seconds, though, ended there. I was ranked last when Mass General sent its intern selection slate to the agency that mixes and matches medical school graduates with residency training programs. I was told during my hospital interview, "We don't usually take residents from *your* medical school. But your letters are strong and your board scores are the highest we've seen. We'll see what we can do."

On a sleeting day in March, I and the hundred other medical students stood nervously in a bland white square room off my medical school main lobby, hopping from leg to leg, waiting to unseal the envelopes that would determine our lifelong fate.

I stood and stared—I had received the same letter of congratulations as the Harvard valedictorian who was ranked first by the selection committee at Man's Greatest Hospital. I was Boston bound. Smiling inwardly, I imagined majestic days ahead, thinking of where I was now and where I would be.

Some of us who would train at Man's Greatest Hospital were internists, some pediatricians, some surgeons. We were called "house officers."

The medical residents, or "fleas" as we christened them—those specializing in internal medicine—were more serious than the others, stumping one another with electrocardiograms and making cases as complex as possible.

We had our ranks. First-years were interns, second-years were junior residents, and third-years were senior residents. Those above them, the recent program graduates who would shepherd us, were the chief residents.

We also answered to the staff physicians—the attendings. The attendings had their ranks too. At the bottom were the assistant professors, then the associate professors. Ahead of them were the full professors, the Gray Hairs, many of whom were section chiefs. At the top of the section chiefs were the department chairs who kept these puzzle pieces in check. Mine was Dr. Donald Ren.

More than schooling and our disciplines, marriage was the biggest class distinction among us. In the beginning, the married ones would sneak home to share newfound experiences with their spouses. As the first year dragged on, wives and husbands grew resigned to partners who were never home, or who while home would be collapsed in dreamland, compensating for long hours of sleep debt.

A few residents had infants, a brutal task with the long weeks and emotional madness ahead. One of my fellow interns, a high achiever from the University of Pennsylvania, kept a locket around her neck containing a blurry photograph of her son. Worn from constant opening and closing, the gold leaf flaked off, leaving tarnished steel behind.

Some of us were jubilant, others depressed. One in our group was so melancholic that a fellow resident and I took turns watching his balcony, fearing we would see him wobbling on its railing ten floors up. He left our group within three months.

My many days of residency and early Boston adventures were spent in the company of my roommate, Wags, a tall Texan who arrived with the expectations of his family's legacy. He too found that his first glimpses of Boston were far from the images he began cultivating in grammar school while reading the Harvard alumni magazines on his parents' coffee table.

He was the son of a famous surgeon whose picture hung in the surgical call room. His father was a Harvard Medical School graduate and had trained at Mass General four decades before. The surgical nurses knew this despite Wags's efforts to keep it private. And when Wags turned in for precious hours of open-eyed sleep, giggling voices would come over the intercom from the nurse's station saying "Goodnight, Daddy" in an exaggerated Southern drawl. They knew Wags saw his father's black-and-white photograph each night before he closed his eyes.

Wags might have come from a rich medical background, but he didn't choose his school for its legacy; he picked the only medical school in the United States with a fraternity. There he thrived, finishing at the top in his class, just as he had in high school.

As a last-year medical student, I met Wags at a conference hosted by his medical school on the Texas industrial coast. Smelling the oil on the ocean, I asked myself why anybody would want to go to school there. He attended my talk, mentioning that he would be headed to Mass General in July and was looking for a roommate.

I wasn't sure how to react to the budding surgeon with arms in slings, a tattered shirt, and a homeless shelter aroma. He explained that while jumping over a tennis net two weeks before, he had caught his foot, breaking both arms in a face-plant fall. For six weeks his frat mates fed and dressed him. Taking liberties, they would dress him in women's blouses, small shirts that exposed his midriff, and shirts they used for wiping spills on the frat bar counter. He took codeine each day so that he didn't have to move his bowels; his friends drew *that* line with hygiene help.

Later Wags took me to a local Galveston bar named Sonny's, famous for a bullet hole in the bar top but more famous for the owner's daughter—blond, smiling, and movie-star beautiful. She must have said "*No!*" a thousand times to the medical students and residents who rocked on bar stools trying to catch her glance to ask for a date.

I didn't choose Rutgers for its legacy or its fraternity. With three brothers in college and grad school, the cost of a private medical school was beyond reach. My father joked that when the tuition payments for his sons were done, "I am going to buy a country."

During medical school interviews at Columbia, Penn, and Yale, I was told, "We will work with you to secure the $150,000 in loans you'll need."

"No thanks." I said. "Five thousand dollars a year in tuition for a lesser name school is fine."

Wags and I compensated for our non–Ivy league universities with hours of studying six hours a night in medical school, all day Sunday too. We worked evenings on the intravenous, or IV, teams to hone skills for our residency ahead and to make a few bucks. Having exhausted ourselves in medical school with tests every Monday and tons of biology to learn, we could now come up for air in Boston. No tests, minimal academic accountability. We just showed up for our hospital shifts and followed the lead on the case.

In medical school, cash went for tuition, books, and fast food. There was no money for fancy dates, just a bit left over for cheap beer. Social events focused on parties after big exams hosted by groups of three or four. As interns, we now had our first income. Across the Charles River, we drove to the now-gone Lechmere's department store, hauling home a twenty-four-inch Sony, the first non-book purchase of our new lives.

On call every second or third night, we cared for patients twenty-four hours a day, sometimes more. The surgeons' call schedule was the most demanding. To have every other weekend off, they would be on call from Thursday through Saturday morning. The next week their call time would last from Saturday at 6:00 a.m. to Monday at 6:00 p.m., and these long hours were heaped on top of call every other day during the week. These days, such schedules remain in lore only, with trainees' hospital work limited to eighty hours per week,

We were tired all the time. Post-call, we fell asleep at red lights, during movies, when lecturers droned. Like horses, surgeons slept on their feet, some tumbling into open abdomens spread with retractors. But our lack of sleep didn't get in the way of our social life. We'd finish call, return to our apartment, read for an hour, nap a short bit, and then, bright eyed, hit the streets of Boston.

For some of our colleagues, getting dates was easy. The young Boston women treated in the emergency ward would slide notes with phone numbers to the handsome surgical residents who were bandaging their sprained ankles or stitching slender fingers cut by broken wine glasses. For others, meeting companions was more difficult.

In Boston for a week, Wags walked downtown to Faneuil Hall, an area door to door with bars. He soon returned, saying, "It's going to be tough here. I told a couple of cute girls at a bar that I was a doctor. They said, 'So what? Everybody in Boston is a doctor. What makes you so special?'"

One needed to look no further than responses to head-on bicycle crashes that happened regularly on the macadam paths along the Charles to witness the Boston doctor glut. Two bike riders would collide and be quickly surrounded by joggers.

"I'm a doctor," one would say. "I'm a doctor" would say another.

"I'm a doctor, "would say a panting third.

Then the next round of pronouncements would volley.

"I'm an orthopedist."

"I'm a cardiologist."

"I'm an ER physician."

"You're a pediatrician. You can go now!" Then my run could continue.

Boston medicine had its own method of Charles River triage.

Our boxes unpacked and bookshelves lined, Wags, the others, and I walked into medicine, Boston, and our limitations. When we took our first steps through the green glass doors, we stood for a moment in the gray granite lobby to glimpse in awe, knowing that our reflections of the years ahead would be impossible to predict.

We asked, "Will we see the diseases we read about in medical school?"

"Will we make the proper decision that determines if someone lives, dies, or is disfigured?"

"How will we cope with the anticipated years of sleep debt and physical exhaustion?"

"Will we be intimidated by the Gray Hairs?"

"Will we have lives beyond the brick- and-granite walls?"

"What kind of people will we be when we are spit out the door when our time in Boston is done?"

The same and different answers to these questions from a pediatrician and a surgeon to be, as different as two medical graduates could be, would come at random, with no set program to follow or eclipse. The answers would come from as many eccentric times out of the hospital as in.

But I had one more question than Wags when my Boston days began: "When my time along the Charles is done, will I still be runner-up?"

Ewald

My first days of medical actions and decisions as an intern gave me a small taste of the days ahead—a heady time to translate what I had learned in medical school to patient care, but also a harsher reminder of what I had not yet learned. It was a time to replace the flippant swagger of medical students, who are told "you are the best and the brightest," with the humility that follows the recognition that we could not doctor alone and that disease could prevail over knowledge. But the arrogance of youth would take years to fade.

Two details that distinguish medical students from greenhorn interns are the "MD" after the name and the courage and ability to prescribe. No metamorphosis of the mind or distinctive wisdom comes with medical school graduation, just more confidence and more respect once the diplomas are handed out. Only a week after the graduation parties faded, I stood amazed that I had patient care and lives in my trust. How did this happen?"

Supervision of the first-year interns varied depending on the senior resident and how compulsive the supervising attending physician wanted to be. Before I entered the Mass General program, my first stint out of New Jersey Medical School was at Cambridge City Hospital, a community hospital on the other side of the Charles River from Boston.

There at night, I was the lone pediatrician. Under my watch was the delivery room, where I would resuscitate purple babies after birth; a general pediatric ward that was never too full; and the emergency room, where the unpredictable was the predictable.

Alone on my first night, a sixteen-year-old girl from a wealthy town in New Jersey was brought to the emergency room severely intoxicated and reported to have taken pills, perhaps Quaalude. She was in town for a summer course for high school students that allowed them to live in Harvard dorms. Seduced by the aphrodisiac effect of Harvard, these young girls were easy prey for Harvard freshmen and sophomores, who would buy them beer and teach them to party.

Calling a parent of a drunk teen in your charge as a physician always elicits the same indignant response: "How do you know that it's my child?" they'd yell at you, followed by shouts of "You're wrong."

In the Cambridge City Hospital emergency room with the intoxicated New Jersey teen and a nurse as green as I was, I dialed my confident and protective senior resident.

"I'll be right there. Don't panic," he said over the phone. "You need to wash out, lavage, the stomach to get the pills and alcohol out. Pass an Ewald tube and irrigate her stomach with saline solution until clear."

I asked the nurse for the tube; she had not seen one before either. We inspected the red rubber tube, half an inch thick in diameter, assuming it was to pass through the nose.

We held the teen, now stuporous. After shoving a gob of petroleum lubricant into her nose, we pushed and pushed the tube until we heard a pop and slid the red rubber hose into her stomach. There was a little blood.

Lavaging her stomach, we washed up pills and soup. The toxicology studies showed alcohol and quinine in her blood. The Harvard freshmen had given her gin and tonics.

My senior resident showed up and stared. "*What!* Rivkees, it goes into her mouth, not up her nose. You probably ruined a twenty-thousand-dollar nose job!"

She was admitted and observed for twelve hours. Her parents hadn't arrived when it was time for her discharge, so the Harvard housemaster was phoned. The girl was still woozy and drowsy, but hospitalization was no longer needed.

The housemaster arrived in a white van with crimson Harvard markings on the side and looked at the groggy girl sitting in a wheelchair. Looking at her puffy face, her hair a mess, he said, "Is this the same girl? Her parents are going to be pissed." I wasn't sure if he meant at him or at me. She was gone; we never heard from her again.

Another entertaining time for emergency room medicine dropped on us when the Grateful Dead were at the Boston Garden. We had acid-laced teens from the Boston suburbs arriving at the ER, spinning, singing, or shouting as we called a parade of parents.

One mother from Newton, a wealthy Boston suburb, cursed us, not believing her son was brought to us on LSD (lysergic acid diethylamide). When she asked to speak with him, we handed the high school star athlete the phone. After he sang, "Orange juice, orange juice, orange juice, orange juice," in LSD psychosis, she reluctantly trusted us. She sped to the ER, her hands cupped over curled lips on arrival.

Seeing her shake, we asked, "Can we get you something to drink?" Her son answered in an "orange juice" refrain until the haloperidol we injected into his buttocks put him to sleep. Twelve hours later he was on his way back home.

At Cambridge City Hospital, I also learned that starting intravenous lines in children was no small task for an intern. With their slight size, dehydration, and wobbly veins, we the inexperienced cringed poking the little ones. I was gratified when my senior resident showed me a pulpy vessel in the neck called the external jugular vein.

"You can use this in an emergency. Hang the child's head off the back of the bed, let the vein bulge, and slide in your IV."

"There it is. It's easy," he said showing me on a pudgy two-year-old.

With the New Jersey teen and her newly bulbous nose still on my mind, a gaggle of infants arrived the next morning, my second day. The sores on their palms and soles and in their mouths meant that Coxsackie virus, a fiend of summer, had struck. Not a typically serious affliction, the virus left infants dehydrated, febrile, and in need of hospitalization.

Unsuccessfully, I poked miniature arm veins to the glares of parents who pleaded, "When is this going to end?" "It's July, you know," the parents said. "He's a new doctor!" As best as it was to defer your illness until the new interns were seasoned, this was just not possible.

"This is no way to go," I said to the nurse who had helped the day before with the Ewald tube. "I know what to do. Ask the parents to step outside."

The next morning, I was the parade master. My charges, three toddlers, were in highchairs in a row in front of the nurses' station, bags of crystalline saline solutions dripping into IVs in their necks.

"Rivkees, I told you that it's for emergencies," said my senior resident.

"Next time I'll get the arm veins," I answered.

After one week of internship, I knew where Ewald tubes and IVs were to be placed. During my second week, I was taught delivery room resuscitation, where the future of infants is determined by rapid responses. I learned to spring to the delivery room and suck meconium, the tarry in in-utero bowel movements, from below the vocal cords of infants who defecated in the womb. We'd slide endotracheal tubes down little windpipes, place them between our lips, suck the feces from the lungs, and spit ferociously. It made me think of Boy Scouts being taught to spit snake venom after a bite. And like that snakebite treatment later shown to be wrong, what we did was later disproved.

My third week into internship, a three-year-old boy named Frankie with small red spots from head to toe and a 105-degree fever was carried in to the ER by his mother. I hadn't seen this disease before, but I recognized it as deadly meningococcal meningitis. With blooming confidence, I slid an IV catheter into the mid-arm and gave hydrocortisone and antibiotics. I *then* called my senior.

The boy was transported to the Mass General pediatric intensive care unit. The spots faded and the boy lived. I felt indomitable. I later learned I was just lucky, as was the boy.

It wasn't long before I learned that medicine builds mountains of humility even more than it builds vast plains of confidence. An intern colleague missed this same diagnosis, thinking it was Coxsackie virus. The child went home to die that night from meningitis. Devastated by the child's death, the intern transferred out of pediatrics. The child was a victim of a deadly disease; the intern was a victim of green insight and thin supervision.

During days when the emergency room traffic was light and when the nights were quiet too, my senior resident would join me on the wards.

We'd talk about physiology and the diseases I was managing in my patients. He directed me in proper Gram staining methods for bacteria identification. We viewed white blood cells by microscope for toxic inclusions, the sign of viral infections. We examined urine samples, looking for evidence of urinary tract infections.

Much of our days, though, were given over to the realization that we were fighting tiny invaders aiming to reach ears, lungs, kidneys, and brains. These predators would divide exponentially, living off the jellies of the host.

I became a part-time epidemiologist four weeks into my internship. Five infants born the previous week came in with rashes. Large red blisters dotted their skin. Some babies had one or two spots; some had forty, along with high temperatures. We knew this could kill children.

Looking through a microscope at the scrapings from these blisters, we could see beefy bacteria in groups of four. We knew the children had scalded skin syndrome, caused by a staphylococcal infection. The newborns were hospitalized, bathed in milky bacteria-killing soap, and given intravenous antibiotics.

We had to find the Typhoid Mary of the nursery who carried the bugs, dropping them like invisible snowflakes on the infants. Naturally, the interns were accused. We were plausible scapegoats considering that we went from the wards to the emergency room, from the delivery rooms to the nurseries, and from procedure rooms to the nurseries.

My senior resident arrived at rounds with a bucket of swabs, each with a number code to protect our identity. We stuck the swabs into our noses, twirling ten times before replacing them in the culture tube plastic sleeve. Off to the microbiology laboratory, the swabs were passed over red blood agar plates to see what would grow.

We weren't the culprits.

Typhoid Mary was Typhoid Paula, a stocky nurse in her forties, with a vocabulary that would make soldiers blush. She would talk about residents, nurses, and parents, saying, "He's a dickhead" or "She's a dickhead," simple and direct.

By final count, she was responsible for the hospitalization of ten babies. She was reprimanded by the administrators, whom she also called "dickheads." She was admonished for not washing her hands between patients, nor after scratching what we imagined were the boils on her ass. Like the infants, she now had to bathe with the milky soap daily for a week and take two courses of antibiotics before she was bug-free.

Three weeks later she was back to her routine, "dickhead this and dickhead that," remorselessly oblivious to the fact that she was the biggest dickhead of all.

My first stint out of medical school done—four weeks of indoctrination with IVs, lumbar punctures, neonatal resuscitation, and microscope bacteria-gazing—I was ready to enter Man's Greatest Hospital. Driving over the Charles Bridge back to Boston and home, I looked down at the water. I could see a reflection of transition from the sheepish mind of a medical student to the take-charge mind of the physician.

Mousetrap

The outcome is seldom good when a mouse head splashes on a brunette's toes—and that was just the start of Wags's and my social missteps. Every long date starts with a small step, or perhaps with a small "snap," I mused.

We rented an apartment overlooking Storrow Drive that had a highway-side sign taunting drivers in the tepid Boston traffic, IF YOU LIVED HERE, YOU'D BE HOME BY NOW. That was close enough for us, thirty feet from the hospital, a short roll out of bed away.

The hospital had a roommate-matching service. Since most of us were making less than twenty thousand dollars per year, pricey Boston rents needed to be shared. Not long out of college and the company of our parents' homes, individual living wasn't for us either.

I was the first to arrive, with a U-Haul of furniture more suited for dumping than unpacking. I had accumulated the decaying discards of my relatives. I had my Aunt Ida's rug for the living room, an American Oriental, once valuable, I was told, though one could see the floor through its thin weave.

I had my Uncle Jack's fading brocade couch. Jack was from Atlantic City, a Dean Martin–like man who wore a smoking jacket. He would cough wildly while puffing away on cigarettes stuck into the end of a shiny black holder. He was a shoe salesman who had come over from Poland when that precious window of escape opened in the 1920s. Jack's couch became the flop site of many residents, nurses, and college friends who would collapse there after long evenings in Boston bars, glad to avoid Storrow Drive at night.

We lived on the second floor above an expensive French restaurant, Maître Jacque. New to blocks of apartments, I went door to door introducing myself. The restaurant owner lived on the same floor and must have been expecting his lover when I knocked. He was naked when his door opened.

The French place below, a five-star eatery, not only attracted an upper-scale clientele but also drew in the rodents of Boston. At night mice would part ways with the crumbs of the restaurant and infiltrate the invisible highways of the building's walls, climbing to visit us.

Our apartment wasn't alone in infestation. Man's Greatest Hospital had mice too, and on some floors the chronically ill would adopt them as nighttime companions. Patients would steal crust from their evening bread and offer their gray friends midnight snacks on the lonely, pin-drop-quiet hospital nights.

Once, a psychiatry consult was phoned in for an elderly gentleman, who was thought to be confabulating about his pet mouse until the floor nurses told his house officer that the man was lucid. The mice weren't hallucinations; they were part of the hospital ambience.

Years later, as a researcher at Mass General, I inadvertently introduced lizards to hospital folklore. We studied lizards by the thousands. Their brains had receptors for the hormone melatonin; I was trying to discover those receptors. They arrived from LaPlace, Louisiana, in boxes stuffed with newspaper that were placed in the hall for disposal when thought to be empty. Time and again we'd hear screams from the neurosurgical intensive care unit next door when the bright green anoles hidden in the packing escaped, scooting into the rooms of men in open-back hospital gowns with wires glued to their shaved heads.

Unlike some of the hospital lonely, Wags and I weren't fond of the mice and set traps and planted trays of green poison pellets in our rooms. The apartment windows, the sliding type with oxidized aluminum frames, let in drafts, so the smell of mice decaying in our walls blended with the Boston harbor air and the exhaust from Storrow Drive.

Jack's couch, we later discovered, proved to be a smorgasbord for mice. Wags's meals were a succession of Stouffer's TV dinners and mine a parade of Banquet brand fried chicken, eaten as we sat on the couch watching the news or a ballgame. A New England blizzard of crumbs fell into the cushions, creating a rodent buffet.

When we dragged the gross old couch to the garbage chute twelve months later, we discovered that the bottoms of the brocade cushions had been infiltrated with mice. The little gray creatures had engineered tunnels and dens to feed and bear their young. A few dead mice were there too.

We upgraded to a couch of fake leather bought from an attending physician in the neonatal intensive care unit. We also bought his weight set, adding unneeded touches of manliness to our living room. The new couch—thick, brown, and vinyl—had no air exchange in the cushions. After guests sat for a while, they'd peel themselves off the furniture, their backs sweaty and shirts soaked.

Even with air-impervious furniture, the rodent infiltration continued. A favored entry point was the wall-mounted heater. Standing beside the rectangular heating unit, we had a splendid view of the courtyard below with its cherry trees, rhododendrons, and azaleas that flowered in early springtime—May in Boston.

Just back from call, Wags was in the shower when his date arrived. Post-call too, I woke from a nap to let her in, seeing the characteristic bug-eyed stare and wrinkled nose of those who caught their first look at our kitchen and living room. On one wall we had a whale harpoon; on another, a crooked pastel Georgia O'Keeffe print. A TV on a nicked wood stand was nearby, but the big brown couch and matching chair dominated it all.

Wags had difficulty parting with used items and had amassed a pyramid of orange TV-dinner boxes in the kitchen, an inventory of consumption. His bathroom had a cache of cardboard toilet paper rolls. Piled on the floor behind the toilet at first, they'd eventually roll down the hallway. He also collected and piled used Head & Shoulders shampoo bottles, dripping with turquoise stalactites.

Wags met his date in a supermarket in the middle of the high-rise apartments. Strange, I thought, trying to figure out the kind of girl who would be attracted to a man with a shopping cart full of TV dinners and anti-dandruff shampoo bottles.

After welcoming the young lady, who managed the accounts for the Charles River Park tennis club, I reassured her that she would be safe. I excused myself to resume needed post-call sleep as Wags was dressing.

Looking at the ceiling and just about to doze off, I heard a "snap." I smiled, anticipating the scream that would follow like a thunderclap follows a flash of lightning. I jumped as the scream broke.

Standing in front of the heater, Wags's date wore the bewildered look of a grammar school teacher who had just been egged. As she was gazing onto the courtyard below, one of our traps unloaded, splattering a mouse on her feet.

If women needed to flee our apartment, which happened a few times, they had two choices. They could turn left to the elevator or, if disoriented, turn right into a putrid garbage room.

Aghast, this girl exited right and screamed again. Wags, done buttoning his shirt, ran from his room to give chase. She calmed down when Wags made a promise to her. Thus Wags's first date in Boston was in the Filene's shoe department, where the cost of a pair of elegant woman's shoes matched his weekly salary.

Seeing how my new friend the surgeon fared on his first date in Boston, I wondered where my first missteps in Boston would take me.

EW Blues

The emergency ward, EW, or the "E-Dub," as we called it, hosted a broad scope of disease and nighttime depravity. We also called the place the "pit."

Today emergency rooms are compartmentalized into pockets of medicine, surgery, trauma, and pediatrics. Yet during our training, those lines were fuzzy. Residents from all the different sections worked side by side, assisting, complementing, and teaching one another. This was where Wags and I learned about quick-action medicine and quick-delivery admonitions.

When serious incidents occurred, such as a pediatric cardiac arrest, the surgeons arrived. When less-serious events occurred, the medical residents—the fleas—ran the show. But we knew no matter how severe the incident, serious or not, if a patient was sick, we wanted a surgeon in charge. The surgeons didn't view the fleas as equals, and we called the intensive care units run by the fleas "Death Stars."

Working in Minor Surgery, where the modest injuries were treated, interns and medical students spent shifts X-raying, splinting, and sewing. You were on call for twenty-four hours, and then you were off the next day. Drug seekers would rotate in and out, complaining of painful ankles, elbows, and knees, pleading for Percocet. "We have something better: Percogesic," we would say, prescribing a mimic that was just extra-strength Tylenol.

Prisoners from the Charles Street Jail a block away, today the location of a posh hotel, visited with cuts, stab wounds, and gashes—some self-inflicted. As we tended to the convicts, the guards would flirt with the nurses or leaf through sport or car magazines that they brought along.

One busy evening a prisoner pulled the gun from the holster of his guard, who was reading at the time. As he walked out of the emergency room, a tiny nurse stepped in his path.

"And where do *you* think *you* are going?"

He stuck the gun muzzle in her face and kept walking. He ran to Cambridge Avenue, carjacked a vehicle, and was never seen again.

The cops also brought pediatric patients. One boy from Dorchester, or "Dahchestah," as he said it, came in with seventy or so one- to two-inch gashes on his arms, face, and chest.

"What happened?" I asked.

"I was jumped by a group of kids. They attacked me with Track II razors."

It could have been worse—we'd seen kids slashed with *non*-safety razors.

One teenager stole a Boston city bus. Buses are difficult to maneuver even for veteran operators. This fellow, just fifteen years old without even a driver's learning permit, steered that bus through Melrose and Malden, eventually crashing in Medford. Sprinting from the bus on the median of the Fellsway, he sprained his ankle. As he hobbled away, a gray-haired officer caught him. The police were still panting from their chase when they brought the boy in to have his ankle tended.

Although we saw only children and teens on the pediatric side, we'd sneak adults in when the adult side of the E-dub was packed. A senior pediatric nurse needed a favor: Her husband had been bitten by a bat. Unsure how the creature took flight in their bedroom, they were awakened by flapping. Her husband tossed his false teeth in the air, knowing the bat would hone in on them. He whacked the black creature with his cane. But as the bat fluttered down, it chomped on his Achilles tendon.

Bats have a high rabies-carrier rate, about 50 percent. The dead bat was brought in too, stuffed into a two-quart Vlasic pickle jar. We started with rabies preventive injections. We stuck two-inch needles into the bite wound, then into the buttocks, then into the arms, delivering rabies antiserum, penicillin, and tetanus toxoid in succession.

The next day the bat would be picked up by the State Department of Health, where its head would be chopped off and its brain stained for rabies virus.

Tired late in the evening, we asked a nurse's aide to put the pickle jar in the EW freezer until the Department of Health could collect it. Joining the many thoughtless actions that happen time and again in the "What were you thinking?" category, she placed the pickle jar on the top shelf of the refrigerator used for medication and juice. Worse, her deed was discovered during a surprise inspection by the Department of Health the next morning.

Questioned by the state official while the hospital was being fined for her mistake, the "I don't give a damn" aide quipped, "The jar said PICKLES."

With a fine pending, the inspectors took the bat to the state laboratory. The head was sliced off and stained. To our relief, rabies wasn't detected. But not only was the nurse's husband out a set of choppers, he had received six unnecessary injections.

Attributed to high volume and high stress, the EW was a scab of ire for the attendings who watched over us. When night traffic slacked and the drunks passed out for the night in doorways, high-rise vents, or downtown benches, we napped on stretchers in the patient care bays.

Some nights when we were busy but the surgeons were sleeping, at 3:00 or 4:00 a.m., we'd tiptoe to the surgical residents snoozing on stretchers and fix locked leather restraints to their extremities, trapping our friends until morning.

Finding his star interns bound to stretchers at dawn's light, the arriving EW attending would yell "Who did this?" waking the sleeping surgeons. There was no answer. We had already gone to the wards or home.

Once we wheeled a locked-down slumbering surgical resident dressed in green scrubs into the elevator of the tallest building of the complex. Deep asleep, he rode the elevator for six hours that night, with more than fifty different patients and staff sharing the ride with him. Reported to be missing in action by the EW attending, he was later wheeled back to the EW, where the strap locks were released.

"Who did this?" echoed even louder.

During slow nights in the EW, spurious referrals slid along the desk of the triage nurse to be handed back with a wink saying, "nice try." Some notes said, "Jack Daniels—alcohol overdose," "Barbara Bush—pelvic inflammatory disease," or "Deborah Smithson (the hospital president's wife)—herpes simplex."

A surgical resident from Utah, who was usually proper and serious, scrawled a note: "Rose Kennedy—leaking abdominal aortic aneurysm." The note was handed to the EW charge nurse, who shuffled backward, reaching into her pocket for a tissue while reading the cryptic writing. Knowing that the aorta can weaken in the elderly and rupture with devastating consequences, she speed-dialed the hospital president.

That Saturday evening, the senior surgeons were attending a black-tie event at the Parker House Hotel overlooking Boston Common. From the hotel ballroom, they could make out the statue of Dr. Morton, who introduced the use of ether in surgery at Man's Greatest Hospital.

The dinner honored the Chair of Surgery for being named "One of America's Great Surgeons." With his recognition he joined the ranks of the distinguished physicians who preceded him. At the award dinner he stood before the younger, eager surgeons who dreamed of the time their fame would earn equally worthy recognition.

The senior surgeons were paged in unison and slid their covered chairs from the banquet table in synchrony. From the hotel lobby they called their answering services before talking softly as a group. They hailed three yellow cabs for a short ride to the E-dub, looking at their watches, guessing the patient's arrival time.

Six surgeons in black tie paced the hospital lobby, tapping their shiny black shoes, waiting for Rose Kennedy to arrive. The ride from Cape Cod Hospital to Boston at night takes ninety minutes with high-speed transport. When the estimated transport arrival hour had passed, the Chair of Surgery asked the charge nurse to ring Cape Cod Hospital.

"I see. I see. I see," she said, lowering the handset with her lip quivering. The hoax was exposed.

But how could the Gray Hairs punish us beyond a yell? Pressed in our work and few in numbers, the loss of one resident was impossible for the program to absorb. When punished, you'd sit and take your tongue-lashing, knowing the blunt words would end and that would be it.

That night the red-faced resident from Utah stood before the Gray Hairs in the lobby. Like the wedding scene from *The Graduate*, when

Dustin Hoffman looks down at the congregation seeing lips rolled back, teeth gnashing, but not hearing a word, the surgeon stood. Then it was over.

He was back in the EW. The senior surgeons hopped in cabs to return to their dinner, which was over by the time they returned. And in the cab rides to the hotel, they all bit their lips while holding hands over their mouths to hide furtive smiles, remembering the days when they wrote such notes.

Evening Interlude

When we were on call in the hospital for our twenty-four-hour shifts or longer, the evenings sped until 9:00 p.m., when we swarmed to the basement cafeteria for the evening meal. The potatoes, molten and gelatinous, fetid brown and yellow, steamed in silver pans. The meat was brown, tinged with green at times. As unhealthful as the food was, we ate it over a fast ten minutes.

We talked intensely over these dinners about our cases and the patients who intentionally or unknowingly tortured us. Shoptalk over, we made plans for the next night. "What game? Who are you going to take?" we asked one another.

We weren't sure why or how, but some of the alcoholics who lived on the street would find their way into the hospital basement to join us for dinner. Perhaps it was part of an experiment to see who could tolerate the food better—the house officers or the drunks. This was a time Man's Greatest Hospital had a soft spot for those who wandered Beacon Hill. These were no ordinary street people. They wore tattered gabardine overcoats; they wore tweed. They didn't dress in the baggy tan trench coats or tattered Army jackets of their New York counterparts.

One of these men fished the trash cans on Cambridge Avenue dressed in Mick Jagger–like black leather. We thought that perhaps he had a syndrome, recognizing the extra-lanky proportions of his El Greco figure. Thin, and menacing, we called him "Psycho Killer," thinking of the Talking Heads lyric "Psycho Killer, Qu'est-ce que c'est, Run, run, run, run, run, run, run away." Like with the others on the street, we knew there was a story behind his fate. Perhaps he was psychotic and wouldn't take his medication. Perhaps his family tried to keep him at home to deal with his mental illness, and when all measures failed, they parted company in tears.

One afternoon, the wife of one of the residents was tossing out her husband's college clothes. "Time to grow up and move on," she said, putting two full garbage bags on the street for disposal. The bags never made it to the Boston incinerators; Psycho Killer ran off with the bags.

Over the next year living on Beacon Hill, the resident's wife sometimes confused the silhouettes of her tall husband and Psycho Killer. She'd jump on Psycho Killer's back—and he'd scream even louder than she did.

The same street people who begged us for money when we dragged ourselves home slept at night in the hospital lobby that housed an old horse-drawn, shiny black lacquer ambulance. A family of Gypsies lived there for a year, also at night, only to disappear at dawn's first light.

Hospital administrators later ended this practice by replacing the forgiving wooden benches with steel-back chairs and metal armrests to divide the individual seats. Even for us, the woefully sleep-deprived, the new chairs were too painful for catching even micro-naps. "Unfair," we said, "to us and to the streeted," and wrote notes of complaint that went unanswered.

We had nicknames for the uninvited evening meal companions. One was "Sputum Man." We never grasped his true ailment, which was surprising in itself, because the fleas provided care for the street people. At dinner we'd watch the fleas debate whether he had focal, segmental, or diffuse bronchiectasis, Goodpasture syndrome, or a rare granulomatous disorder. Wags and I wondered whether he had a family, where he grew up, if he went to college. Always there was an untold story for the man on the street. Considering his nastiness and his habit of spitting at the good-natured nurses who cared for him, we guessed his story was not pleasant.

But as Sputum Man's food went down, his sputum would come up. Not into the neat, crisp, folded, starched handkerchiefs that the distinguished Harvard physicians tucked into their tweed pockets. His sputum came up by the cupful. At the start of each meal, he'd arrange three or four plastic cups like toy soldiers. He would then fill usually two or three of those cups with bubbly green sputum that was ejected between forkfuls of food.

As we exited the cafeteria, we kept our distance, afraid to catch tuberculosis or whatever other affliction he might have. Even the Gypsies stayed away from Sputum Man. But when we walked by him, some of the fleas would also slide him cards with clinic phone numbers.

A likely victim of his nasty lung disease, or perhaps taken off the streets by the police, Sputum Man was suddenly gone one evening, and so were his rows of putrid cups.

The Gypsies had foretold that something bad would happen to Sputum Man. "He was cursed," they said. Fearing his curse lingered after his departure and would transfer to them, they quietly parted ways with us too. Forever after, the lobby would be empty at night.

Plans for the next day set, gossip over, ten or twenty minutes gone and meal consumed, back on our paces we went.

Fenway Fondness

As Wags and I came to accept being called "doctor," our off-call time revolved around women and baseball, mixing and mingling the two. The Red Sox found their champion legs well after our first year in Boston, when they were mired in mediocrity.

On weekdays, after Friday call nights, we'd trek to Fenway Park. On an intern's salary, we could only afford the four-dollar bleacher seats and two-dollar beer. Parking was never a problem, as the stadium was usually half full. We were rookies, along with Roger Clemens and Oil Can Boyd, that year.

As a rookie, Clemens showed the early dominance of a star in the making. Fans stuck big red Ks on the Fenway-green bleacher walls with every strikeout. To avoid an unfortunate-looking KKK three strikeouts down, the last K of the three was turned backward.

What Clemens had in heat, Boyd had in personality. With the zaniness of a maniac, he would sit in the bullpen, gyrating and jabbering, or pace as the others sat calm, spitting sunflower seed shells. Later, Boyd said he was coked out of his mind in his Red Sox days.

Wade Boggs, the young Red Sox third baseman, was left unprotected on waivers that year, and no other team claimed the future All Star. Several years later he went for the money, departing Boston for Yankee pinstripes, a move that irritated the Fenway faithful. Forever afterward he was a "loosah." And when he returned to Fenway, he was greeted by the Boston mantra of "Yankees suck, Yankees suck, Yankees suck."

The bleachers in right field at Fenway that summer were filled except for one area where "Mongo" sat, so named by us for the bulky cowboy in

Blazing Saddles played by Alex Karas, who rode an ox and knocked out a horse with a solo punch. He sat in the center of an empty ring of seats, no one within ten rows out of fear. He rocked, gorilla-pounded his chest, and yelled at those who came near, "Get outta here, *now!*"

He would then yell "Har, Har, Har!"

Wanting to take advantage of spacious seating, after ten games we befriended Mongo. We never learned what he did for a living, whether he was connected with the Boston mob or not, though it looked like he could be. He only told us that he had a brother in the Navy. As we inched toward the vacant seats near Mongo, we tried to reassure our dates that Mongo wasn't rabid as we calmed them with beer. Fearing Mongo, they sat on the edge of their seats. Mongo was a good luck charm though; the Sox never lost when Mongo attended.

One hot summer night, Boston was playing the Detroit Tigers; nine triples rained, most of them hit by the Sox. The Detroit outfielders feared the large man they saw leaning over the outfield wall. Approaching the Mongo seating area, they'd pause as they ran—and singles and doubles stretched to three-base hits.

Post-call on humid summer days, we'd be asleep in our seats by the fifth inning. We'd wake for the fights that were plentiful in the cheap seats then. Usually, overmuscled guys would say the other team sucked, triggering swings. After tumbles with stadium police down the concrete bulkheads marking the exits, the men were tossed out of the park, not arrested like they would be today. After the game, we'd see them chugging away at the Cask 'n Flagon, one street away.

One Kentucky Derby day in early May, Wags and I headed to Fenway. We were to pick up a girl living on Beacon Hill whom Wags had met the night before at Daisy Buchanan's, a neighborhood bar. She was from Minnesota and moved to Boston to work for State Street Bank.

"She's really nice," Wags uttered in his Southern drawl. Heading down Cambridge Street, Wags spotted her just as she was waving us down and flashing a toothy Midwestern smile.

"My God, *she's obese!*" he yelled at me. "What do I do?"

"Didn't you know this?" I replied.

"No. She was sitting down," he said.

Doing the right thing, he stopped the car and she hopped in, with the curse of a lower torso that dwarfed her upper half. Distracted by the upper-half misrepresentation, Wags parked his car near the McDonald's across from Fenway but forgot one essential thing. As we walked to the ballpark, a young boy jumped from the bushes behind us.

"Hey, mistah! You left your engine running. I'll get your keys out for ten bucks!"

So we paid.

At the season's end, we saw an arrest photo of that boy in the paper after he was caught breaking into cars during ballgames. But the day we met him, he was on the side of decency, helping us when he could have driven the blue Cutlass to a chop shop.

As we matured in Boston, so did the Red Sox. They won sixty games in 1982, seventy in 1983. In 1986 a bold leap brought them to the World Series versus the New York Mets, and we went to all the playoff and World Series games played in Boston.

World Series game five at Fenway was religious. Smokey Robinson sang "The Star-Spangled Banner" and segued into "America the Beautiful." He and his singers, with large gold bangle earrings, sat near us behind the first-base dugout, listening to the park resound with driving, taunting chants of "Darryl, da-da-da Darryl!" directed at outfielder Darryl Strawberry's apparently very thin skin—the Sox fans proud to be part of the distraction that affected his play. The Sox had a 3–2 game lead in the series as they headed to Shea Stadium. Two days later, Mookie Wilson's slow-rolling grounder trickled through Bill Buckner's wobbly ankles, and hopes of Red Sox salvation were over until seventeen years later.

The girls of Fenway wore a standard uniform of tight blue jeans, long white T-shirts topped with a blue Red Sox jersey, and ponytails sticking out the back of team caps. Some of these girls were the Cathys I courted my first summer in Boston. One Cathy worked at Macy's, one at the hospital; one was a friend from college, another I met jogging along the Charles. The Cathys recognized that Wags and I chased the Sox and spent our precious free summer days at Fenway. But if a Cathy telephoned before a home stand looking for game company, Wags never asked for a last name, complicating my summer.

Not all the Cathys liked baseball. Some were fonder of the Boston Harbor evening booze cruises on bland fat, white boats where wine and beer were served in small plastic cups that cracked if you laughed too hard. Sitting on the stern of the top deck, one Cathy opened her pocketbook to put on lipstick. All her purse contents spilled out onto the deck below; to her embarrassment, condoms floated down along with the makeup.

Wags, the Cathys, and I spent lots of time at Faneuil Hall our first summer in Boston. One of our coresidents, a young surgeon who was as pale as the starched hospital whites we were given to wear, became so legless on nights out, we couldn't get him home. Three times, we put him to bed on the bench in Faneuil Hall on the arms of the life-size bronze statue of Celtics President Red Auerbach. Red watched over him during warm nights. At first morning light, the surgeon straightened himself out, tucked in his shirt, and marched up Cambridge Avenue to Man's Greatest Hospital.

Another hot summer evening, Wags and I headed out for the downtown bars. Two days before, he had contracted a virus that caused head-spinning vertigo. With patients coughing in your face, or sneezing or stooling on you, we were forever getting ill. This was one of twenty viruses that year.

"You need to see Greg for some meds," I told Wag. Greg was a neurologist in training, identified as "wicked smart." From the Deep South, he was the lone person at the hospital to wear a short-sleeved doctor's coats.

Wag didn't recognize the name of the medication Greg handed me with the admonition, "Whatever you do, tell him not to drink while you're taking this stuff!" I didn't know what it was either, but I suggested he double the dose.

We made our way to Cheers, our neighborhood bar (its real name was the Bull & Finch). Later the TV show of the same name would put a dent in the local quaintness. Buses would pull up to the wooden door, and middle-aged men and women would push to have their pictures taken in front of the bar sign and plop down the steps to buy T-shirts and sweatshirts sold at the door.

Wags met a nice girl that night. I remember seeing them dance, her hands feeling his every pocket for the hidden condom of his intentions. Knowing the game, Wags stayed a step ahead, rotating the latex from pocket to pocket to avoid getting caught. Not finding a telltale foil packet, she smiled and said, "You're a nice guy."

I met a girl that evening whose father owned a food supply company; she was up from Providence for her bachelorette party. The next week she was going to marry a boat builder twenty years her senior—for the money, I guessed.

The next morning, Wags overslept for his shift and was awakened by the harsh rebuke of my senior resident on the phone. "Where are you? Get your ass in here *now!*"

Dressed in a minute, he was rounding in five minutes, dizzy and hungover in the surgical intensive care unit with twelve unstable patients.

"Are you all right?" asked his senior, noticing that Wags was wobbling and sweating.

"I'm, I'm, I'm," he said, trying to finish his thoughts. Then, within the bug-eyed view of intubated patients, his charts fell and he let loose beer-based vomit that splashed onto the intensive care unit floor, backing up with each heave.

He was put on a stretcher and rolled next to a young man in kidney failure, who looked over and smirked, "You look worse than me." An IV was placed, saline was given, and Compazine calmed the retching and put him to sleep.

"What was in that stuff the neuro resident gave me," Wags asked me after the resident stopped in to check on him.

"I told you not to drink," I said laughing. "See ya at dinner tonight."

"Yeah, right!" he answered. Five hours later, Wags sat up refreshed, yanked out his IV, and resumed his twenty-four-hour-call shift.

That afternoon he endured the sideways glances of the parents of patients who had witnessed the morning show. They felt bad for him, never questioning his ability, thinking he had contracted one of the million germs riding the air currents in the unit, coughed out by the infirm.

Recovered and rounding that afternoon, he heard one of the patients say, "Doc, how are you feeling? We were worried about you. You need to take better care of yourself! We need you!"

The ignominy of that summer hit me too. A light sleeper, I was usually aroused easily from call-room sleep, but not this time. After the evening meal, the duties of the pediatric intensive care unit that night done, I went to the call room at 2:00 a.m. for sleep.

The staff banged on the door for who knows what, but I couldn't be wakened even when they shook me. "Perhaps he was out too late last night," the charge nurse said. "Poor fellow," said another with a wink.

The next morning after refreshing sleep, I glanced at my feet. My toes had been painted with methylene blue, a dye that works its way deep into protein and DNA. It took three months for my digit discoloration to fade, and I got tired of being asked "What happened to you?" I wore socks and sandals at the beach and told any who asked that I was European.

In spite of our early-summer setbacks, with the black print on our noses from too much studying over too many years beginning to fade, Wags and I realized that to move beyond the cloister of school, we would need to walk out of the hospital as much as we walked in.

Free of the repression of medical school, ready to make up for my long-delayed socialization, this was the start of off-call times dappled with humiliation. This was the beginning of the essential insanities that made us sane.

Night Moves

Not that we didn't have freedom of thought and action during the day, night was when the wards truly belonged to us. The fate of those in our care was in our hands—the young, the supercharged, the sleep-deprived.

Details of the day's events, the pending lab tests that needed follow-up, and the unique caveats of the hospitalized patients were passed on to the covering team. Some house officers passed along their index cards, so full of scrawled data that they looked like dictionary pages. Others penned notes on napkins that found their way to dripping noses. Others fashioned elaborate notes, using markers of yellow, blue, and green.

Most evenings unfolded the same—a page from the EW about an admission, and then the dance of the residents' night would begin. Down from the sixth floor, with medical students in tow and clipboards in hand, we'd ask the same questions the physicians in the EW had asked, repeat the same exams done an hour earlier, and write the same orders written in the EW. Then the pressure came to move the patients upstairs to alleviate the EW bed crunch, a perpetual problem as old as the hospital.

Before we could authorize an admission to the floor, we had to wait for a junior or senior resident to arrive. Wise and knowledgeable, their one- or two-year advantage over us translated to a decade of experience we lacked.

There were several different kinds of juniors and seniors.

There were the "timid seniors" who did whatever we suggested, offering to start our IVs or write our orders.

There were the "oppositional seniors" who would do the opposite of what we suggested. If we wanted to admit a child, temperature 105, red cheeked and vomiting, they would say, "It's scarlet fever. Send him home."

If we didn't want to do a lumbar puncture, they would say, "Stick a needle in the child's back."

Then there were the "wall seniors" who resisted admission at all costs. No one ever seemed sick, even when presenting with a stiff neck and photophobia, the signs of meningitis. "Send the child home" was the admonition. Thus, against our nascent judgment, the sick child and irate parent left.

Most of the time the children sent home did fine. Yet occasionally there was the "bounce," the patient sent home from the EW who would return the next day to be admitted with a serious problem.

The bounce of infamy transpired on a Saturday evening on one of those wonderful cobalt-sky days of Boston summer. Flying from Kansas, the parents brought their one-year-old, who was neither little nor cute. Born prematurely with immature lungs, the child developed a bizarre inflammatory lung disease. We wondered if his lung disease triggered the production of hormones that caused him to bloat to incredible proportions, with pillowy cheeks.

The infant, who had a green oxygen mask that looked like a spot on his large face, and his parents were ushered into an exam room. The parents pulled his medications from a grimy, opaque plastic bag.

"We're here to be admitted," they said. Then the dance began.

My senior was from the South. He went to Harvard as an undergraduate, followed by Harvard Medical School, followed by a Harvard residency. We called him and the others, who took this hallowed Harvard path: "Preparation-H's."

"I know you have come a long way, but I see no reason to admit your son." Seeing resistance from the parents, he said, "Yes. I understand your frustration. But your child will do well at home. Y'all should fly back home tomorrow." Making these pronouncements over the background noise of the child's snorts, wheezes, and gurgles, he then turned and walked away—conversation over.

"How can this boy go home?" I muttered to myself. But that was the power of the senior.

Escorted to the street, the Kansas family ambled to the Holiday Inn on the next block over. They pushed the stroller holding the infant, dragging a green, nicked-metal oxygen tank behind. Secluded in their hotel room, they made phone calls.

The next morning, the child returned. This time, a directive came from the top.

"Admit this child! End of discussion. Do you or do you not understand?" Dr. Ren had spoken. The bounce of infamy, the child stayed with us for two years.

Two years is a long time to live in a hospital. His care involved tens of doctors and hundreds of nurses. Caring for him, we scratched our heads, trying to solve the mystery of his massive cheeks. We measured what we could, making up names of new hormones in his image—cheekatonin and jawastatin. We collected and banked his serum and urine for the genius scientists to use to uncover the problem.

Sadly, the boy from Kansas never again saw the light of day, never got to smell the salty Boston Harbor air or smell the fresh-cut Kansas hay. He died of influenza, caught from one of the other sick kids on the ward.

On the night he died, his parents were still en route back from the Midwest. His death imminent, he was rocked by one of the nurses until his heart stopped. We, the house officers, came to see our friend giving one last touch to his forehead as he died. When his pulse stopped, his mysteries faded along with him.

On call in pediatrics, there was constant activity. Tending to the pediatric wards, we threaded IVs into veins as thin as chest hairs, looking up doses of Tylenol and ampicillin and other antibiotics for the feverish young. In the early-morning hours, we looked at X-rays and stained fluids and pus.

The surgeon's life on call was harried too, devoted to checking blood gases for blood oxygen levels and preparing patients for surgery, including emergency cases. Unlike the pediatricians, who kept no written records of the hundreds of children we cared for, the surgeons noted case specifics in a special log to be completed after each operation.

The later it got, the busier we all became. Offices closed, parades of toddlers were sent to the EW by the community pediatricians. The occasional dehydrated, toxic, and wilting child was admitted. With the routine came the rare, left to the wise senior to uncover.

Another of my early lessons in the humility of medicine came five weeks after my first rotation in Cambridge. A teenage mother arrived in the EW with an infant that was fussy and not nursing well. We started the IV, drew cultures, and put the needle in the back to collect spinal fluid—our routine for sick infants.

This night, the Compulsive Senior was on. The Compulsive Senior had a stack of note cards rivaling the guestbook at the Statue of Liberty. The Compulsive Senior left nothing to chance or trust, inspecting the child like a stamp collector gazing at a rare discovery with a magnifying glass.

There was a single, clear, tiny blister on the tip of the infant's nose. The Compulsive Senior pushed me out of the way, notified the intensive care unit, and next telephoned infectious disease specialists. Radiology was contacted to arrange for an emergent CT scan of the brain.

I stood back, dwelling on what I perceived as the Compulsive Senior's gross overreaction. Within eight hours, the infant was seizing uncontrollably. The CT scan showed holes in the brain that expanded and joined as we watched the images appear on the screen.

I recalled that the only other time I had seen movement during a CT scan was in a rotten-tempered veteran from a nursing home in Chelsea—the city on the other side of the Tobin Bridge from Boston. He had a head roll of gauze covering a scalp abscess that was blamed on a cane fight with another mean old man. When the roll was taken off, we saw flies. We next saw maggots on his scalp. The CT scan of static images captured movements of the tiny worms swimming below his skull.

Within sixteen hours, the infant was stiff. Herpes virus was devouring her brain in a way that I would have never imagined, but the Compulsive Senior had predicted this course. The following morning the girl was alive, but with a brain laced with holes.

"How do you explain this to a teenage mother?" I asked.

The Compulsive Senior did that. He was as wonderful with the grieving parent as he was with his brand of medicine, which I forever after tried to copy.

I won't be runner-up if I can be like him, I thought.

One week later, the baby was taken off life support. I read her two-line obituary in the *Boston Globe*.

Night call hit us each differently. Some of us seemed to have a nuclear motor that powered us throughout the evening, with lectures given at midnight to medical students, pounding into their minds the information we thought they should know. There were also the after-midnight discontented, circles under their eyes, speaking in gibberish long before their shift was over.

These were the ones who declared, "I just don't care." They trotted to call rooms with beepers turned off. Others wouldn't disengage their beepers, though it would have been better if they had, because their work was robotic, without thought or insight.

I'm not sure how many calories we burned on those nights. It must have been in the thousands. We'd sneak into the patient nutrition rooms and take cans of chalky Sustacal or other high-energy drinks, supposedly invented for astronauts but now used to supplement nutrition.

We'd steal an hour or two from our work to lie in call rooms on light-green plastic mattresses, the same type used for incontinent patients. We'd wake with leg cramps, at times confused and not knowing where we were. Hospital sleep was never sound.

Occasionally we'd carry the "code-call beeper," the first line of response for cardiac arrests. Just having it on our belt ensured poor, one-eyed sleep. The responses to our alert beepers or the phone in our rooms had to be instant. A ring, a jump, a run. It took years to extinguish my jumping behavior when the phone rang in my home at night.

Nighttime was when the young and elderly would die. Sometimes the staff died too. There was a wing of the hospital for the rich and famous—the Bullfinch Building. Presidents, senators, actors, poets, kings, and queens stayed there. Floor-to-ceiling sapphire tapestries hung on the walls. Tea was served in the afternoon, and private-duty nurses chatted in a lounge with Monet-style oil paintings.

The private-duty nurses hired by the patients for extra attention were older than most of the hospital nurses. Hired through agencies, their credentials were unknown to us. One of these nurses meant to give an old man a back rub with Eucerin cream, a great tonic for dry skin. Grabbing the wrong tube, she instead coated the old man's back with nitroglycerine paste, used to dilate the heart vessels of those with angina. The man's blood pressure fell to zero. Thinking he was napping peacefully after a soothing back rub, she missed the signs of death. "He died so peacefully," she said in a soft English accent.

One night on the wing of the rich and famous, a gentleman who owned a software company rang his call bell twenty times during the night. Knowing he had a private-duty nurse of his own who was paid double that of the recent graduates working the rest of the ward, his calls were ignored with indignation.

The next morning the fleas found the gentleman stuck in bed, eyes wide open, looking at the private-duty nurse in rigor mortis in the embroidered chair in the corner of the room.

During the day, there were too many people around for the sick to die. Even the young seemed to want a private and quiet death. After the visitors left and the halls were silent, the cardiac arrests and sudden strokes would creep in. It was their time, their way.

One night when Wags was on call, he was summoned to the emergency room to admit a gray-haired man, sixty years old, with abdominal pain. It must have been three or four in the morning, the time of dead-dog tiredness. Wags sat in a steel chair, interviewing the man and recording his medical history.

Earlier in the year, we wrote long detailed notes. As the year wore on, our notes became short and cryptic. Showing how cryptic one could be, one surgical resident became so disgusted with the workload, he shortened his notes to the date, a checkmark, and his name. The yells and threats of the Gray Hairs failed to change the ways of the "Checkmark Surgeon."

But this was early in the year; the transcribed history was long, and Wags was thorough. When the EW attending arrived at 6:00 a.m., Wags was found asleep in his chair and the gentleman he had been interviewing was dead. Wags had written six full pages before falling asleep upright. Who knew when his charge had died?

After midnight, as we did more, our attention span became less. One exercise that transformed us into clinicians those long nights took place in the "microlab," or microbiology laboratory. About the size of a partitioned toilet stall, it was as disgusting as a gas station bathroom on a highway.

The microlab was in the back corner of the emergency room—a fetid suite where great diagnoses were born. Like Sabbath wine, the staining solutions of our forefathers were housed for our reverence: hematoxylin, eosin, methylene blue (the cause of my summer of stained toes), Gram stain solutions, Parker pen blue, Sudan black, potassium hydroxide, ferrous chloride. Anything that made a color and could be squeezed into a plastic bottle was on two dirty shelves in random placement.

We stained everything that came out of bodies, be it liquid, solid, or molten. The more it stank, the higher the yield. Spinal fluid, urine, pus, feces, and vaginal drainage—we stained it all. After midnight, we swirled the drippings on small plastic bacterial dishes filled with gelatin agar with shades of red. On these dishes we'd culture the offending tiny bacterium or fungus. Our plated samples found their way to the main hospital laboratory the next morning—weeks of antibiotic therapy and survival dependent on our work of the night.

At night, peering into the microscope, lenses filthy, we'd see phantom objects not there. Sometimes bugs were there but were missed because we were too tired. Other times when we were plating samples, the code-call beeper would go off and away we sprinted, leaving open patient samples on the counter, gone when we returned.

You'd identify the type of code by the sounds of the response team. Pediatric teams wore sneakers at night; their codes sounded like the start of a road race. The fleas wore leather-soled shoes; their codes sounded like the opening of the stock market. The surgeons wore wooden clogs; their codes sounded like horses galloping over Boston's cobblestone roads.

With a sneaker code called, up six flights of steps we ran. Of the countless codes, I still recall one involving an infant in ventricular tachycardia arrest, already undergoing compressions and bag-mask ventilation by the time I arrived.

Pediatricians affix cute items to their tools to lift the spirits of kids, but usually they only make the care providers feel good while spreading germs along the way. Stethoscopes had tiny koala bears or Disney characters pasted on. Gumbys were twisted around the silver handles of otoscopes. The photos on our identification badges would be superimposed with stickers of Snow White, Donald Duck, or Larry Bird.

Running the code, I was eye level with a baby girl whose face was obscured by the ventilation mask. One ID badge, not from our hospital, caught my eye. It was the image of a man with big eyes on the edges of a head that was wide at the top and narrow at the bottom. Following lidocaine, epinephrine, and several joules of electricity, the infant's life was restored.

I peered up to see the presumed prankster, surprised to see that the man's face matched the badge. The father had a rare genetic condition, Crouzon syndrome, which he had passed on to his daughter. The father worked at night to hide his looks. Now he wanted to hide his tears of guilt, recognizing that his genes were killing his next generation.

On the move throughout the night, with the approach of dawn we'd make time for just thirty minutes or more of quick sleep, which seemed so much longer. After half-hour naps, our brains recharged, we had another ten hours of work ahead. On those post-call days, we dozed during morning report, during rounds, during lectures. It was the constant motion and the tasks ahead, not the caffeine, that kept us going. When the clock hands reached 6:00 p.m., our night and day came to an end.

The married went home and slept beside their bored spouses. We, the unmarried, slept for a brief time, read a little, regained our energy, and were soon on the streets of Boston. The next morning as dawn arrived, glad to have slept in our apartment, Wags and I walked across the street and did the dance all over again.

The Pink Shirt

With the march of months of training, the distance between the house officers and attendings narrowed. The younger attendings, many of whom had only recently been through what we were going through now, took us under their mentorship. And within this embrace, I learned that the attendings were as quirky as they were kind and knowledgeable.

An outsider, before arriving in Boston I imagined the venerable Harvard physician as a gray-haired New Englander with a starched white coat and a serious, deliberative demeanor. But that wasn't their way. The faculty was as much international as Boston. Hardy students, survivors of academic Darwinism, and foreign medical school graduates found their way to Man's Greatest Hospital, where those who excelled remained.

One of the attendings from France carried an unlit walnut pipe. Approaching the bed of an ill child, she would say in a nasal accent, "What does this child need?" We would toss out the names of drugs, trying to best one another.

"*Non!*" she would pronounce. "This child needs a pillow! He looks uncomfortable. Get him a pillow!"

Well versed in the medicine of medicine, the attendings could step back to focus on the issues that were important to the child or parent, issues invisible to us. I learned that if a patient came to see you with an unsightly goiter and a rash that bloomed the day earlier, you had better address that rash before the goiter.

The attendings watched over us mostly from a distance, knowing that to grow we needed independence of thought and time alone in our deliberations. They were not the constantly hovering attendings of today's medicine that house officers come to expect—the ever-present crutch that compromises curiosity and self-reliance.

Early in the academic year, the chief residents paired us with the attendings we were to work with us as mentors, crafting bonds that could be eternal. Those interested in respiratory medicine were paired with experts in asthma or cystic fibrosis. Those with interests in cancer were paired with oncologists. Those curious about the bowels were brought under the tutelage of gastroenterologists.

Endocrinology and metabolism attracted me. Thus I was matched with a group of physicians as eccentric as they were smart. These doctors, the soul of my training, would pull me from my assigned rotations to attend their lectures or see children with rare disorders. Each of these attendings was unique in his reputation.

"Dr. Bigelow is a horrible driver," it was said.

"Dr. Peacock is disorganized and very British. If he takes you out, he will make you pay for parking," others noted.

"Dr. Yogur is brilliant and will make you salsa dance," said a few.

They had their pecking order. Dr. Bigelow was a professor with distinction and section chief. Dr. Peacock was an associate professor hoping to make professor. Less than ten years removed from training, Dr. Yogur stood in the assistant professor ranks.

Each of these three was special in his measured way, and each would shape my career, showing me the humility, brilliance, creativity, and pleasure of medicine.

Dr. Bigelow was the most elegant and brilliant physician I would encounter in my career. A gentleman's gentleman, he opened doors for ladies and let those younger pass before him. He hung his coat on a hanger instead of throwing it on the floor. He had a lightning-fast wit, mulling over words just uttered by others and responding with clever wordplays.

When he answered questions, the insight of decades of knowledge— his and his mentors—rolled out in perfect prose. An explorer, he looked for the explanation others couldn't find. He searched for the better treatment, the novel explanation underlying a child's disease.

He revered his trainees with brains, potential, and energy, pushing them to be better than they thought they could be. Those with less aptitude were treated politely, never made to feel that he had favorites. And when his trainees moved up the academic ladder, they became his colleagues and friends, confidants for complex case discussions.

Dr. Peacock was a tall, barrel-chested man, and his name matched his personality. He was from London. My images of Englishmen were of stodgy, stiff-upper-lip chaps. But as I learned from Dr. Peacock and the other Brits I met over the years, they loved to laugh and joke over both good beer and bad.

Dr. Peacock had room-filling charisma. When he walked into a room of people, those present would flock to him. They'd listening to his stories of his complex cases and his international travels. He had lived with pygmies of the Ituri Forest. He examined effects of opium on growth of children in Afghanistan. He said he characterized thyroid function in sharks off Bali.

With the insight of genius, he peered at patients through a unique lens, coming up with questions about the condition never asked before. He wasn't as detail oriented, though, when it came to his own person.

He'd arrive to see patients with one shoe brown and the other black. He would wear his wife's cat's-eye reading glasses, leaving her to look though his brown plastic frames that day. He matched his socks by thickness.

Dr. Peacock never smoked around his wife, only around us. With an office in the burn center, he had to light up on the sly. Dr. Bigelow knew this and would knock on Dr. Peacock's door when he suspected smoking.

One morning, Dr. Bigelow opened the door without a knock and watched Dr. Peacock discreetly tuck his lit cigarette into his coat pocket. Dr. Bigelow deliberately extended the conversation until he stood to say, "Your jacket is on fire," as he left for the hallway.

Each of the endocrinologists taught in his distinctive style. Peacock educated through excitement and off-guard questions. He would reach into the front coat pocket of his coat to pull crinkled sheets with laboratory test results printed on them. He would pass the pages to me and ask, "What does he have?" I never knew.

He challenged conventional wisdom. "Dr. Bigelow thinks this boy has pseudopseudohypoparathyroidism. It cannot be. What do you think the boy has?" he asked me. *How would I know if Dr. Bigelow didn't?* I pondered.

He would ask me to review manuscripts sent to him from *The New England Journal of Medicine* for a thumbs-up or thumbs-down opinion. When I thought the reports were great, he showed me the flaws. "They don't know what they are talking about," he would say.

He asked me to assist him in writing test questions for pediatric endocrinology board examinations. Then he'd rewrite my questions to start with the phrase, "It's malpractice to use which of these treatments?" The answer he selected as correct was usually the treatment used by the rest of the country's physicians.

When he'd ask me to review the second-opinion cases that came his way, he would ask me, "What does the patient need?" I'd name a few tests to run. "No." he would say. "What this patient needs is a *doctor!*"

Dr. Yogur too had a great heart for those on the way up. He was a master teacher, the best I had, and I copy his style and still use his lecture content today. He'd invite us to his salsa parties that lasted until the early-morning hours, unless his neighbors rang the police before the party's end.

He was from Colombia and had come to the United States as a Fulbright scholar, first living with a family in Oklahoma and not knowing any English. Ambitious, he found a way to train and stay in the United States, working his way to Mass General.

"Let's talk about growth," he would say, and he would lecture for an hour, just me and him, challenging me as Dr. Bigelow had done with him. "How come you don't know that?" he would ask. "Didn't anybody teach you that?" Such admonitions pushed me.

He made me draw steroid structures on the board when he knew I couldn't. He gave me articles torn from the journals he read and quizzed me three days later about their content. He made me teach the other house officers and medical students, knowing that the true way to learn was to teach education through education.

I had heard that when Dr. Yogur was in training, he went with Dr. Bigelow to a lecture at Brown University, sixty highway miles south of Boston in Providence, Rhode Island. Upon arrival, Dr. Yogur was so ill from Dr. Bigelow's jerky clutch that he was admitted to the emergency room for treatment with intravenous fluids and Compazine, missing the presentations and case discussions.

Dr. Bigelow demanded much of Dr. Yogur in training. He required presentations about complex patients, that five journals be read per week, that letters to referring physicians be composed.

At one point Dr. Yogur lost his libido. Fearing he had developed hypogonadism, he snuck samples of his blood to be tested for low testosterone in the hospital laboratory clinical sample runs. Hiding his intentions, he'd tell the laboratory technicians, "These are for a friend." When his testosterone level came back above normal, he boasted his result to Dr. Bigelow, whose response was to ask even more of Dr. Yogur.

My attending folklore stories would bloom too. Excused from my morning work by my senior resident, I was invited to accompany Dr. Peacock, who was going to deliver a lecture about water balance and antidiuretic hormones at the University of Massachusetts Medical School in Worcester.

As Dr. Peacock drove, he smoked and weaved through traffic, making abrupt lane change without turn signals. His driving was welcomed by middle-finger salutes and shouts of "Ya bastahd."

The smoke and the to-and-fro swerving left me nauseated and red-eyed after the hour ride. "Are all endocrinologists such bad drivers?" I asked myself. Pulling into a handicap-parking space, speaking in his strong accent, Dr. Peacock looked at me and said, "You're not going to have to go to the emergency room like Yogur, are you?" Then he laughed.

"No. I'm fine," I replied, wanting to heave.

Within the stark auditorium, two hundred physicians and trainees had gathered. I sat in the first row as Dr. Peacock was introduced. The host talked about where Dr. Peacock went to college and medical school. He mentioned where Dr. Peacock had residency and fellowship training. The host told a few jokes that were received with polite laughter. He described Dr. Peacock's great discoveries, how Dr. Peacock proposed that extracts of cat spleen could cure hyperthyroidism in women but cause hypothyroidism in men. I felt proud being in his company.

Standing while being introduced, Dr. Peacock turned to thank his host while his first slide was projected. The text was a description of a child with a complicated water balance disorder. Results of the tests performed were shown next.

Pointing at me, he queried, "Rivkees, what does this patient have?"

I froze. How could I be expected to answer questions in front of hundreds? How could I comment on a subject I was completely ignorant of? I blabbed something that was so disjointed it sounded intelligent. "Good," he responded as he rested his palms on the podium.

He next reached into his pocket and pulled out a pack of cigarettes, tapping out one, lighting it with a match, and then drawing a few timed puffs. With each slow puff, his presentation seemed even more deliberate and significant.

As the slides flashed by, the smoke around the podium drifted, adding to the dramatic flair. He next began to stride before the screen. Then the surprise of the moment hit me in the jaw.

Dr. Peacock was dressed in a tight gray suit. Fond of pastel-colors, he wore a heavily starched pink shirt. Before going on stage, Dr. Peacock had jumped into the men's room. After relieving himself, he tucked himself inside his trousers; however, four inches of starched pink shirttail jutted out, caught in his pants zipper. These four inches of pink stood erect like a wind-whipped flag on a Falmouth beach.

Back and forth he paced, pointing at slides, puffing away. The audience began to murmur, first those in the front, then those in the back. Then stifled laughter was heard as a few trainees and attending pointed. One smartass aimed a red laser at the shirttail.

When the fifty-minute lecture ended, Dr. Peacock took a few questions, taking a puff to think before each answer. When done, he was thanked for a "most memorable lecture." He then shook hands with his host saying, "Your crew really pays attention."

I was a first-year intern. How could I tell a distinguished physician why the audience was so locked on? Thus, like his smoke clouds, I let the tale of the pink shirt drift off into the lecture hall.

Soon on our way back to Boston, forewarned, I paid for parking and tolls. Luckily, gas wasn't needed.

The pink shirt lecture was just the beginning of my special times with Dr. Peacock. I had a confidante who would help set the course of my career. I dreamed that this was someone who could take me from runner-up to front of the pack.

We talked about endocrinology, sodium, and thyroid hormones. He told me how he came to train at Man's Greatest Hospital, then the top pediatric endocrine program in the country. He told stories about how he and his wife traveled around the Northeast and Canada in a rusty Volkswagen Beetle, tracking patients with rare forms of diabetes insipidus. They slept in tents on muddy farms. At meetings, he introduced me to the experts who authored the books I read.

With his help I overcame my often-paralyzing nervousness of respect, which kept me from speaking with the Gray Hairs. "You need to get over your state-school inferiority complex," he would say to me. But he also knew this complex was the motor that powered me, and he left it there to percolate.

While I was being groomed for an academic career within a few months of my Boston arrival, I saw reflected in Wags's eyes that surgery was a less-nurturing order than pediatrics.

The Gray Hair surgeons were very tough on their trainees. All missteps among the surgeons-in-training were known at the top. Falling asleep holding retractors or taking a history in the emergency room from a lifeless patient wasn't good. Black marks were recorded in personnel files. The surgeons caught screwing up in the ORs had notes stamped "Confidential" placed in their files. The surgeons who injured their hands in out-of-the-hospital activities were flagged.

When the young surgeons became despondent from night call, deaths, or mistakes, intervention was rare; it wasn't the surgeon's way. Pats on the back, utterances of "good job," were seldom. Academic Darwinism, survival of the fittest, was at play.

I observed that much of what we learned in the hospital was horizontal, passed from resident to resident. But I recognized that to succeed, I had to learn from the ranks above. As my friends in surgery were having their pride trimmed with oral scalpel slices, my career would move along, guided by attending friendship.

My special bonds with Drs. Bigelow, Peacock, and Yogur would evolve over the years when they taught me to approach rare cases, each of their styles supervening the others'. They forced me to overcome my exhaustion and submit presentations for national meetings. They put me on the hospital stage to be recognized for my efforts.

And as the bonds with my medical fathers grew, I became ever more grateful, even if the reflection of some of these bonds was forever tinted pink.

M&M

In medicine, *M and M* stands for "mortality and morbidity." Not this time. The mystery began with a strange crunch. Post-call Wags shuffled to the kitchen trying to decide which Stouffer's TV dinner would be the evening meal. Along with Aunt Ida's tattered American Oriental rug, in the living room we had a plush mauve carpet, a remnant bought somewhere in town.

With each step, there was a crunch. Not the crunch of a cockroach or a desiccated mouse underfoot; it was the crunch of a peanut M&M. Reaching down, he found a yellow peanut M&M, then a red, then a brown, embedded in the nylon pile.

"What's the deal?" Wags said looking at me. "Why are you putting M&Ms in the rug?"

I was with one of the Cathys, hysterical, laughing at Wags as he crawled the length of the room plucking nuggets from the broadloom. I professed no role in the chicanery.

On days when we weren't on call, Wags and I would run five to seven miles along the paths that flanked the Charles. With the peanut mystery looming over us, we talked as we ran later that evening, perplexed, about the candy in the carpet.

When we ran, I'd take the pace out quickly, but Wags always finished strong, passing me at the last curve along the riverbank to the IF YOU LIVED HERE, YOU'D BE HOME BY NOW sign. We ran so often on our off days that we made the background footage of the weekend news four different times. We'd later train for marathons, finding time for long-mileage days among high-mileage work hours.

Mostly we ran late afternoons or early evenings. After call, though, we'd sometimes sleep till 10:00 p.m. and then run. At night, the asphalt and pebble paths along the Charles were beautiful. The wideness of the Charles made a thick, black silhouette against the night sky. The flashing white light of the MIT dome reflected on the flat water, and cars' headlights rippled.

Nighttime on the Charles was a bit weird, though, especially the area near the Hatch Shell, where concerts played on summer weekends. Here the Boston Pops played the "1812 Overture" to cannon shots on the Fourth of July. This also was where weird men perched at night. Sometimes offers of sexual favors were chanted as my pace slowed at the end of the miles.

At the end of one nighttime run, I was approached by a skinny bald man who said, "I have a bottle of champagne. Do you have any paper cups?"

"You've got to be kidding," I said, "But you're original!"

Run complete, dripping with sweat, and back at our apartment, we discovered yet more M&Ms in the rug. We scratched our heads trying to finger the colleague who would do this, as several house officers had keys.

Wags had a date that night with Dana, a nurse who worked on the surgical floor. Dana was an Angel of Death. One year earlier, jogging in Summerville, where she rented a small house, she came upon a dead body under an overpass. Six months earlier, she was the first responder to two car accidents where drivers and passengers had been killed.

On the wards her death luck was a bit better, but there she was prone to concentration lapses. Once she gave Mama Maria, a diabetic elderly Italian woman, an overdose of insulin. Thinking she was testing Mama Maria's urine for glucose, she instead tested a cup of apple juice she had placed on the *right* metal fold-out arm of the red medication cart. In error, she placed Mama Maria's urine on the *left* arm of the cart—areas reserved for juice and medications.

Hearing one of her patients scream after a gulp, she gasped at her mistake. Retreating into the solarium where Mama Maria was parked in a big brown geriatric chair, she found Mama's face covered with soot—she had eaten an ashtray's contents in hypoglycemic delirium.

That night, Wags and Dana went out. Taking a break from my routine, I went out with a non-Cathy. We each told our dates that we suspected the other of planting the M&Ms in the carpet. I was off to Fenway Park; Dana and Wags were off to a restaurant requiring a jacket and tie.

Wags, truth be told, was blessed with more heart than social grace. The waitress delivered bread and a carafe of wine to the table. Believing the carafe was a wine stein of a sort he had indulged himself with in medical school, Wags picked up the glass urn and chugged down the wine, muttering, "This is gooood!"

While in medical school, the carafes Wags drank from weren't made of polished glass. They were the quart-size plastic urinals that are hung over hospital bed rails, a common feature of fraternity life. But Wags was no longer cloistered in that life of amusement, where a wet burp counted more than a "please."

We'd each been on dates that ended abruptly, like a steel door slammed closed by a strong arctic wind. As Wags emptied the carafe, his date-door blew shut, finally sealed by a coat-sleeve chin wipe.

Dana nodded politely here and there, doing the best she could to hide the glances at her watch. Before dessert came, Dana said, "I forgot. I have to work at eleven tonight."

"How could you not have known that?" he asked.

"I just forgot," she said.

With the inconvenience of the long work hours came the "beep myself out" convenient excuse. We could "beep" ourselves out of any predicament we were trapped in. We were on call so often that when we said, "I'm busy tomorrow, Thursday, *and* Friday," it was always believable. This sword cut two ways, though, as the choir of nurses knew our tricks and played the game too.

While Wags was busy exuding Southern charm on Dana, I was at Fenway with a nurse I had met in the EW. Once in an abusive relationship, she talked about the sad things that had happened to her. Episode one: She told me about being thrown downstairs. Episode two: She talked of how her car was once set on fire. Episode three: She described how her ex-boyfriend got her best friend pregnant. Episode four was the story of how he tossed her off a porch. Then my beeper went off.

Pushing back from the restaurant table, Wags was now wiping the gravy off his chin, getting ready for a hasty retreat back home to accommodate Dana's shift. Back at the apartment twenty minutes later, Dana reached for her car keys, which she had left on the kitchen counter next to the Stouffer's boxes. As she leaned forward, looking through one of her short shirt sleeves, Wags saw light from the other side—the "air sign" of the flat-chested.

Doing his best to continue to impress Dana, Wags paused in earnest thought. He'd just finished two weeks on a plastic surgery rotation and appreciated the marvels of breast implants. He recognized their different shapes, their varied sizes. He knew their consistency when squeezed lightly, softly, or strongly.

Not perceiving that the 11:00 p.m. work deadline was feigned, Wags said, "Ya'll know what? You'd look really good with bigger breasts. I'm doing plastics now. I could help yooou."

This time, the real door slammed as Dana turned her back on Wags and huffed out. Wags stood there innocently confused. "What? What did I dooo?"

But Wags *knew* she'd be back. Exiting right, not left, she was now standing in the garbage room. She guessed that he'd pursue her, but the battle between self-pride and hygiene is a tough one; at that moment, she had more pride than hygiene concerns.

Refusing to open the door after Wags's knocks, she kneeled on the slimy floor, peering out the door-bottom crack and watching for him to leave. When it was past 11:00 p.m., Wags knocked again.

"Y'all gonna be late for your shift," he said.

"Thank you for your concern," she said.

"Can you get me a glass of water?" she then asked. When she saw him walk into his apartment for a glass, she sprinted out of the garbage room to the nearby steps, taking deep breaths to clear the rude odor from her lungs. Seconds later she was in her car, and blue smoke came from her Mustang's rear wheels as she drove off.

"I've got your water," said Wags, reappearing with a smile. He found the garbage room empty but fully fetid.

When I walked into the living room, Wags was sitting on the brown vinyl couch drinking Dr Pepper, eating peanuts, and watching the replay highlights of the Sox game I had left in the third inning.

He began laughing, not at the thought of Dana in the garbage room but at the discovery of a new cache of M&Ms buried in the carpet.

Among Wags's proclivities for Stouffer's TV dinners, Head & Shoulders shampoo, and Dr Pepper was his love of nuts. Each night he ate a can of almonds, cashews, or mixed nuts. In the top drawer of his bedside table, he kept nuts in reserve.

Wags and I watched the Sox game to the end, not sharing our tales of the evening. We each retired for the evening.

As memories of Dana faded, Wags made a discovery the next morning. Sleeping with the window open on one of those days when the wind blows in from the east and you can smell the ocean, Wags was awakened by a soft rustle.

A fat squirrel sat on his window ledge. Both eyes open, Wags lay motionless, watching the gray vermin hop into his open nightstand drawer. The squirrel chewed through a bag of peanut M&Ms that Wags had tucked under ten pairs of white socks. The squirrel stuffed two M&Ms in his cheeks and darted into the living room to bury them into the carpet pile. *That is one resourceful squirrel,* Wags thought, wondering if the squirrel had been tipped off by our mice.

Running back into Wags's room the squirrel hopped onto Wags's bed, jumped to the nightstand, and then jumped out the window. He perched on a tree a few feet away, looking back at Wags as Wags looked at him.

The phone rang, sending the squirrel in flight.

"Wags!" It was Dana.

Not intending for me to hear him, I heard him tell Dana "I'm sorry. I'm sorry."

He wasn't apologizing for the evening. In fact, he thought the night went well and he believed she was calling to tell him about the terrific time she had.

At midnight, on her way home from her date with Wags, Dana came upon a crash on Interstate 93 north. A financier who had just finished a long week of work had stopped to change a flat tire. As happened all too often, he was hit by a swerving drunk. Her death-discovery count was now five.

Gray Hairs

Man's Greatest Hospital had a caste system. We at the bottom were the Untouchables. Those at the top were the Brahmins, not unlike the Beacon Hill Brahmins, legacies of Boston wealth and tradition. Those in the middle, the junior faculty, were closer to us than the top. Several had graduated from our ranks no more than ten years before and were now trying to establish themselves for a leap to the next level. When Wags and I first walked through the green glass doors on our first day of work, we struggled to imagine how we would interact with the cognitive giants.

The scholars at the top, with gray hair or just bald domes, walked slower than us in short, white coats—the blazers of the institution. They talked slower than us, having learned that the slower the cadence, the more respected the word. They spoke less than us too, no blabbering or word inflation.

Some had more hair on their eyebrows than on their heads. White hairs would jut randomly in one- or two-inch locks above wrinkled eyelids. Occasionally eyebrows would be twirled and waxed on the ends, framing a severe look.

I dreamed of sneaking up on them with trimmers when they napped during conferences. I'd lop off hairs longer than one inch; they would never notice. I dreamed of legislation mandating the trimming of eyebrows with all haircuts; a quick razor buzz, and presentations would be enhanced. Those who made the laws, though, were a bushy-browed lot.

There were also those with hair on their ears, coarse bristles of gray hair perpendicular to the helix. Some of them resembled schnauzers. *Let's add ear-hair trimming to the bill too,* I thought.

Few had beards. Perhaps they didn't have the time for beard grooming. Perhaps it was a generational phenomenon.

Although gray hair was commonly at the top ranks, gray hair hit our ranks too, both men and women. The girls would color theirs; the men wore their gray temples as badges of distinction. It didn't help bring more respect—we were ranked more by our postgraduate years than our looks.

Our ties were from neck to belt. They were stained, out of style, and contaminated with bacteria, fungus, and viruses picked up from the microlab and patients. Bow ties weren't for us, and those of us who wore them were chopped down with ridicule—not for the look but because they were clip-ons. The skill of knot tying had not been passed on by their fathers or grandfathers.

The Gray Hairs' bow ties, on the other hand, were real; they were perfectly positioned, knots midline, wings even. *In the time it took to fix the perfect knot, they could have trimmed their eyebrows to public standards,* I thought. Some would alternate long ties and bow ties. The reverent stayed with the short form, day after day, chevrons on their neck.

Even with their seniority of years, their faces wrinkled from decades of thinking and problem-solving, kyphotic from osteoporosis or from bending over open abdomens—"the surgeon's slump"—they worked long days like we did. They were in at 7:00 a.m. and out at 7:00 p.m. They were in on Saturday and in on Sunday, tidying clinic notes, reading journals. I wondered if they mostly waited for us to knock on their doors for advice. But, intimidated, we seldom did.

Admittedly, I was intimidated by Dr. Bigelow. It took a decade after I started my training before I could relax enough to fully learn from him—a decade of regretted lost time. Such was the penalty of my ways, which pushed me to overachieve in some areas but held me back in the face of legend.

With brilliant blue eyes, he inspected all spoken and written words with amazing insight. Those eyes also sat below unruly hedges of eyebrows. He spoke with the cadence of Jimmy Stewart but was even more deliberate—each word perfect, each word filled with crucial meaning.

Even when he rebuked us, we first thought it was a compliment. With the replay of his words, we saw otherwise. Once, I was asked about a patient's calcium level.

"It's 8.5," I said.

"What's the total protein?" he asked next.

"I didn't get one," I answered.

There was a long pause before he spoke again. "I would think that someone with your intelligence and good schooling would have ordered a total protein."

Was this a compliment or a rebuke?

It was a rebuke.

Other times my tongue would seem to swell when I spoke with him, my words nonsensical, nervous logorrhea.

"Tell me. What does insulin do?" he asked.

My answer cited more than twenty different hormone actions. "There were effects on cellular transporters, effects on cell growth, and effects on gene regulation," I rambled.

He answered, "It moves glucose into the cell." No word inflation—just the clarity of simplicity.

Like the other senior staff, he was at his desk every day. When snow blanketed the area, his Subaru beat the orange snowplows to Boston. He would wait at his desk for us to show, chat about the Sox, or talk about case. Those who didn't suffer the nervousness of respect talked to him, but they were few.

Along with the deliberation, he had a great sense of humor. Two years later, I was applying for fellowship for advanced training in his program. I flubbed my interview. He said he would let me know the following Tuesday whether I'd been accepted.

When I called I said, "I've been itching under my skin waiting to speak with you."

"Well, I am glad to be able to end your formication problem. We are glad to have you join us!" he replied.

I'm not sure whether I ever felt completely comfortable with Dr. Bigelow when I started training with him. Eventually I learned to slow my thoughts and ask the right questions. I recognized that his legacy was the sharing of transgenerational knowledge. Books, reports in journals, and conferences were no match for his decades of experience with the common, odd, and unknown cases.

Even those at junior levels knew to tap the knowledge of those ahead of them, knowledge learned from years of questions and interactions. There was gentle challenge as well.

Dr. Peacock was a master at this. With deferential respect, he would draw in his breath and ask Dr. Bigelow, "Tell me what you think about this case?"

Recognizing the trap, Dr. Bigelow would say, "That all depends. What aspect?"

When the opportunity presented itself, Dr. Peacock tried to get an upper hand, especially when a laugh was around the bend.

Once Dr. Peacock invited Dr. Bigelow to the room of one of his patients. "I'd like you to examine this boy I've been struggling with. Perhaps you have seen this before."

Dr. Bigelow stood at the end of the bed, asking the young man precise questions that didn't reveal much.

"Do you mind if I examine you?" he asked.

First he examined the head and neck with the deliberation of a stamp collector. Then he inspected the torso, noting freckles in the armpits and dark marks on the back and chest that looked like drops of spilled coffee. But Dr. Bigelow jumped back when the boy dropped his pajama bottoms. Dr. Peacock was smiling and biting his lip, a perfect setup. Front and center was a penis that reached the boy's knees, the consequence of a growing neurofibroma. Covering the boy back up, Dr. Bigelow said, "Thank you. It was a pleasure to meet you."

Down the hallway, Bigelow and Peacock walked, quietly laughing together. Dr. Bigelow said, "I know what he has!"

"So do I!" said Dr. Peacock.

My department chair, Dr. Ren, of the "did you or did you not's" that would come later, was another high-ranked Gray Hair; he directed an operation that was an academic ant farm. Faculty, trainees, nurses, administrators, and other staff were under his eye. Patients, faculty, and support staff stuffed complaints into his inbox. He, in turn, rotated his attention to the house officers and faculty aspirants—the subjects of letters from discontented families.

Our chair made us feel valued and as though our opinions counted. The "problem children" were taken under his wing as well—those who couldn't make decisions, those who pissed off families, and those who committed serious mistakes. He put us ahead of the entire faculty, including the money-counting administrators.

As the leader of our department, each week he introduced the grand rounds speaker, who addressed the department about new developments in medicine. Some speakers were residents with the courage to educate the rest of us. Some speakers had won Nobel Prizes; others were hoping to win a Nobel Prize.

During these lectures, the Gray Hairs sat in the front. We took our seats in the back so that we'd be less conspicuous when our heads bobbed in instant sleep. Near the podium, the Gray Hairs slept more than we did, sitting with eyes closed but no head bobs. Occasionally their snores were broken with a gentle elbow. Yet after the talks were over, they would ask insightful questions, as though their sleep had been a smokescreen. Perhaps their eyes were really open, obscured behind those hedgerows of eyebrows.

Not long after my training was completed, Dr. Ren had a sudden heart attack one winter day while exiting a Boston subway on his way to work. To the woman giving him CPR after he collapsed, he was just another man on the street to be saved without a second thought. She had no inkling that the man receiving chest compressions—and who would die on the street—had saved the lives of a hundred children and launched a hundred careers that would save a thousand more. Dr. Bigelow later died of a stroke in his sleep, his wife beside him. After he died, I still called his office on Saturdays and Sundays, not wanting to believe the reality, hoping for one last "Hello. This is Dr. Bigelow."

After their deaths I felt an emptiness that still lingers within me. There would be no more weekend discussions of perplexing cases, which were Trojan-horse excuses to talk about nothing important. They would not be there to advise me about the difficult career direction questions that would later arise.

I now answered my questions alone, realizing that, all along, they had answered my questions by holding a mirror to reflect my questions back at me. I now held the mirror alone. And as I did, I wondered why the mirror felt so much heavier now that I held it than when they did.

What We Know Now

The early times of our career blended with the early times of new diseases, or diseases that had been around for a while but had gone unrecognized. This was the time when the other trainees and I did not know what we did not know, as Donald Rumsfeld would say. In the early 1980s we were to face new and ominous challenges.

As a medical student I occasionally saw cases that stumped those with gray hair and long white coats—as physicians at most medical schools, certainly the school I attended, are distinguished from the medical students, who wore short white coats to the waist.

I always believed that coat length was a ridiculous badge to mark levels of seniority. Taken to the logical extension, I imagined assistant professors with coats to just above the knee, associate professors with coats to midshin, and full professors strutting in white coats with tails, wearing white linen gloves in place of latex.

But at Man's Greatest Hospital, every coat was short. It was said that we were all students and that students and faculty were to push each other—a belief that came from the confidence to say that we knew far less than we thought we did.

The first person I learned to take blood from was a man from Haiti, about thirty years old, hospitalized with recurrent spiking fevers. With each temperature elevation, we poked a two-inch needle into beefy veins in his forearm and drew five to ten cubic centimeters of blood, which we rapidly transferred into bottles of a special nutrient-rich soup for growing bacteria. One bottle was for aerobic culture; one was for anaerobic bacterial growth.

The other students and I took turns with the blood testing, sometimes sticking the fellow three times a day, until no veins were left for the poking. Each culture came back with the test results: "No growth to date." It was the medical student's dream, the quest to identify the fever of unknown origin, or "FUO."

We drew blood without training. "See one, do one, teach one," is the motto of medicine. No gloves, no personal protection, no needle protectors like those used now. I know I pricked my finger drawing his blood, as did others. Back then we were more embarrassed than personally concerned, so self-sticks went unreported by some.

We drew antinuclear antibodies. We tested complement levels. We sent blood for serology to the Centers for Disease Control in Atlanta to detect rare viruses. All results were negative as the gentleman slipped into a feverish, emaciated condition.

When you're hospitalized and the medical team is stumped, you find that you stop getting attention. You sit in bed watching TV or read if you have the energy. Your family visits a lot in the beginning. After weeks, though, the cards and the room-brightening flowers don't make their way to bedside tables anymore. But with the influx of new medical students, case interest reblossoms like the geranium in a barbershop window that gets watered once a month to live a little longer. With new short coats on the wards, medical head-banging and case interest becomes alive again. And at last we spotted it. On the roof of his mouth, halfway back where the solid meets the soft, we saw a lesion—a small ulcer, furry and white. Culture tubes in hand, we swabbed the spot, transferring its contents into media to detect tuberculosis, bacteria, and fungus.

We visited the microbiology lab three times a day until we were shut out by the lab techs. Hospital laboratory personnel sometimes have little tolerance for residents. As far as medical students were concerned, we were pests to be ignored.

Compounding the lab techs' disdain for students, as we made our discovery, another crisis loomed on the ward. The number of narcotic pills delivered to the dispensary didn't match the number that went into the plastic medication cups. New to the floor, we were accused; each of us was questioned, one at a time, by two administrators looking for the drug seeker among us. Three days later one of the floor nurses was nabbed, her locker packed with tablets of codeine and vials of morphine and methadone. But we were the ones accused; we were the ones not trusted.

This was just the start of my encounters with medical narcotics abusers. One of my fellow pediatric residents was caught at the lone hardware store on Beacon Hill trying to copy the EW narcotics cabinet key. The store owner recognized the stamped code on the key and, saying he had to go to the back room to get a different blank, alerted the hospital police. That resident left the program for a month-long detox program.

One surgical resident would order two hundred Percocets for discharge pain management for each of his patients. Saying he was completing the circle of care from admission to discharge, the surgeon would push the nursing staff out of the way, insisting that he alone should give the discharge instructions. "After all, I caused the pain, let me fix it" he'd say.

Smelling a rat among the hospital mice was an insightful nurse recently graduated from nursing school. Just out of school, she still wore her white nursing cap with black piping, ends bent like terrier ears. She asked to look at the patient's pill bottle while the patient and family stood waiting for the slow, stop-at-every-floor elevators. Looking in the bottle, she saw ten tablets, not the two hundred shipped from the pharmacy.

She nervously reported her finding to the charge nurse, who kicked the complaint up the ladder. The resident was suspended for three weeks. His suspension was a blessing, as the outcomes of the rare instances of medical staff drug abuse could be far more tragic.

Not that we read the obituaries regularly, but occasionally we flipped through them looking for the names of those in our care, sometimes startled instead to recognize a colleague's name. Once I saw the name of a young anesthesiologist who had pushed self-medication too far, like the ether-sniffing physician in *Cider House Rules*. Early one morning in another hospital in town, about three years after we left Mass General, he was found dead on an OR table, a ventilation mask over his face connected to the nitrous gas tank.

Trying to put the false accusations of our narcotics pilferage behind us, we were back on the FUO hunt. Aspergillus, an opportunistic fungus that hitches onto those with weakened immune systems, grew from the Haitian man's palate ulcer. Yet, even with fungus in hand, we all remained stumped; more experts were consulted. Yet the more we talked, the more the fungus grew, until it invaded the man's sinuses, blood vessels, and heart, killing him. I did not know it then, but this was my first sight of the human immunodeficiency virus (HIV).

The same time we saw infant after infant with a bizarre type of pneumonia that was smothering these children. On respirators, breathing tubes inflating their lungs, these babies were dying. Lung biopsies were performed at the bedside. Small cuts were made on their chest; lungs would pop out like miniature pink sponges, to be snipped and placed in culture tubes.

An infectious disease specialist was called in to consult. "PCP!" he yelled. "It cannot be!"

Pneumocystis carinii was another parasite that affected those with damaged or immature immune systems. Again, the cause was unknown. Years later, I realized this was my second peek at HIV.

The diseases of my medical school, at that time in the early 1980s, hadn't walked through the doors of West End Boston yet. Man's Greatest Hospital, however, was seeing another disease—one new and weird.

From New York and the shoreline of Connecticut came boys and girls with red, sprawling rashes on their legs, backs, arms. Some of these kids had meningitis. Some had wrists swollen the size of softballs.

To Boston these children came for the Gray Hairs to crack the case, and to be hospitalized for weeks of antibiotics. A group of scientists from Yale soon discovered the culprit: *Borrelia burgdorferi*, the cause of Lyme disease, named for the Connecticut town where many of the infected lived.

Inevitably, the disease that hit the palate of the wasting man I cared for in medical school and infiltrated the lungs of the just-born soon made its way to our wards in Boston. A slight four-year-old girl who had moved to Chelsea from Haiti a year earlier was admitted with repeating fevers and weight loss.

She had a walnut-size lump on the right side of her neck next to the angle of her jaw. The Gray Hairs arrived and said, "It's tuberculosis."

That month I was working on the surgical team, as it was mandatory that the pediatric interns do a rotation on surgery. The whites and khakis of pediatric were swapped for the green scrubs of surgery. My every third night on call became every other night. I walked taller, saying, "To cut is to cure."

My surgical senior was neither a timid, oppositional, nor compulsive senior; he was the "proper senior." From the Deep South, we talked of Faulkner, quoting lines that reflected his mood of the moment. We reminded him of the Northerner's view of Faulkner, saying, "On the night Mama discovered what Pa had been doing to sister, little Joe was eaten by the hogs." Biting his lip, he would smile in proper fashion; no dignity of response was granted.

During my time in the faded greens, I was paired with a real-deal surgeon in training. Full throttle with desire to become a cardiac surgeon, he needed a stellar and unblemished residency record to snare the brass ring of heart-valve training. Sensing the vulnerability of his ambition, we had opportunistic fun with the "Cardiac Kid."

Our attending surgeon that month was a brilliant woman with short-cropped hair who specialized in complex urinary tract disorders. Most of the cases would start off with a metal scope stuck in the urethra of an anesthetized child to survey nature's faulty plumbing.

This was no ordinary device; it was a two-headed cystoscope manufactured by Amish craftsmen deep in Pennsylvania, we were told, a perfect tool for teaching. It looked like a two-headed snake, with each head an eyepiece we peered into. My co-intern would peer into the scope, being directed by the attending to look up and down at this and that structure. I stood against the wall awaiting my turn—the interloping pediatricians always looked last.

The Cardiac Kid and the attending surgeon were bent at the waist to peer through the cystoscope, just enough to expose the top of his scrub pants. There was just enough space for me to empty two eight-ounce tubes of clear, goopy ultrasound paste into his greens. As I had my fun, he swatted at me with one of his hands and, in the process, jiggled the scope.

"Why aren't you paying attention?" yelled the attending, her scrub nurse laughing under his mask, knowing what was at stake with her rebuke. Another swat was followed by another rebuke, and the Cardiac Kid saw his prize fellowship slipping away. Finally, he stopped swatting at me. After two more tubes of the paste filled his scrubs, he let the goop run down his legs—a small price to pay for the storied career that lay ahead.

During my time as a surgeon, I learned the importance of eye shadow among the scrub nurses. Clad top to bottom during operations in blue gowns, blue shoe covers, and blue caps, all that remained to distinguish one from another was the three-inch gap from the bridge of the nose to the forehead. The eyes of OR staff thus became the flag of surgical courtship. Eye makeup was as much an art form as brilliant surgical technique and could bend the thin line of courtship from misery to glee.

Like the embarrassment experienced by two women wearing the same dress to a wedding, such was the shame of shared eye shadow color. Boston department stores, aware of their medical-field clientele, arranged special eye shadow counters. YOUR SCRUB NURSE NEEDS MET HERE! read the signs at the makeup counters at Jordan Marsh and Filenes.

I learned that surgery was like golf. There was neither talking on golf course greens nor idle chatter in the OR. Unaware of surgical etiquette, my times in the OR were sonorous, filled with talk of ball games and nights out. During an appendectomy I assisted on, a chunky scrub nurse with green eye shadow came from the adjacent suite to yell at the Proper Senior and me.

"*Will you shut up!*"

Standing in the background for several weeks, my lone independent procedure—the culmination of two months of "scut" and retractor holding—awaited. I was to remove the neck mass from the girl with the fevers and wasting illness.

Several months earlier, competing scientists in France and the National Institutes of Health in Maryland had identified the virus that ravished the immune system of the affected. One named the virus HTLV-3, the other called it HIV, for human immunodeficiency virus. Only the scientist from France received the Nobel Prize for the discovery.

Standing in OR3, the Proper Senior looked at me and said, "This is your case. Tell me what you want me to do. I'll be your assistant."

Surgery looks easier on TV and from the back of the operating room than up front. But an hour later, the lymph node was out, an olive-size, pulpy mass that felt like a frozen carrot.

We bisected the mass, sending some fragments to Pathology and some to Microbiology. Nothing grew from the cultures.

"Who did the biopsy?" the Gray Hairs asked. Fingers pointed to me for the failure of culture growth. Finger-pointing stopped, though, when a sample sent to the National Institutes of Health lab showed that HTLV-3 was present.

A few months later, when I was back on the medical side of pediatrics and out of my surgical scrubs, I cared for this girl. When her sister came down with the same disease, we cared for her too. Today HIV is a chronic illness treatable with antiviral drugs. Then HIV was new on the scene and was usually fatal.

The girl developed a rare tumor in her spine, from which she died. Her sister died four years later. Her parents died the year after they lost all their children. As they were dying, I imagined them saying, "We will soon see our girls again."

With the discovery of HIV, the way we practiced our avocation changed overnight. We played in blood. We started IVs by the hundreds with bare hands, drops of blood getting on us with each stick. Surgeons even compared the number of blood spots on their white shoes, worn proudly like medals. They scoffed when told their shoes were gross.

We now had to wear gloves—to earnest protests. "How can we feel those tiny veins?" we asked.

We no longer performed mouth-to-mouth resuscitation. "Wait for the code cart to get here," we stammered.

Precautions came into effect to reduce the risk of needle sticks when we did blood cultures or stained fluids in the EW microlab. We were now potential targets of a virus that could infect us with one tiny slipup.

And tiny slipups, the hazards of our manual labor, happened. One pregnant pediatric intern stuck herself with a needle of an IV drug user who refused to be tested. She carried a cloud of fear along with her unborn child until enough time passed for her to know that she and her child weren't infected.

A senior surgeon operating on an HIV-infected man nicked his thumb with the scalpel. He ripped off his gloves, ran into the next room, took a fresh scalpel to his thumb and, anesthesia free, excised the tissue along the stab wound, something he knew was wrong.

We saw friends and coresidents die of AIDS, the disease caused by HIV. Some were in pediatrics, some in medicine, and some in surgery. Fearing that I had jabbed myself when I was first sent to draw blood from the withering Haitian man, a time when I was too ashamed to report the incident, I let years pass before I got tested for the disease. I couldn't admit to myself that I too might one day suffer his fate.

Summertime

A hot weekend at the tail of summer, Wags and I were off call together. That Friday evening we went to the bar in Back Bay where Wags met the girl with the little top and big bottom. Jim Rice, a Sox outfielder, stood there trying to look inconspicuous, which was impossible. We had chatted with him before in Boston bars where at times he sat alone, people unaware of his celebrity. This night, though, he was holding court, young girls rubbing up to hear his stories of over-the-shoulder catches and three-hundred-foot throws to home plate.

Ballplayers were commonly seen in town during Boston summers. Visiting teams' players weren't known to the locals, allowing them to blend in anonymously. Once, the Abbreviation Resident, whom I will write about later, and I sat next to Yankee players at Houlihan's Restaurant in Faneuil Hall. Plastered by the Red Sox that weekend, Goose Gossage, Don Mattingly, and Bobby Murcer sat in a booth, no words spoken between hamburger chews. In person, they seemed smaller and less physically defined than the athletes we saw on the field.

We thought about asking for autographs. But seeing them so sullen, we left them alone. So did the other patrons, and no gadflies shouted "Yankees suck," the unifying Boston anthem.

With Jim Rice co-opting the bar attention that night, Wags and I walked to Cheers, a mile away, where we did the hit-and-run. We'd walk up to women, who would turn and run.

There were Cheers regulars who fared better than we did meeting women. One of the most successful was a man in his mid-thirties or early forties, with a thick mustache and shaved head, who looked like a member of the Village People.

One morning while out for a jog around 9:00 a.m. on a Saturday, I saw this fellow lying on his back on the hood of a car on West Cedar Street in Beacon Hill. He was asleep, snoring, with his penis sticking out of his pants.

An irate young woman approached him yelling, "Wake up. Wake up. You're disgusting!" Still drunk, he didn't respond to her yells. I kicked his feet a few times until he awakened. He looked down at his pants, tucked himself in, and dashed off. In the heart of Beacon Hill, he had apparently had a liaison the night before on the hood of the car with a girl he met at Cheers.

I'm sure a few people had heard the late-night happenings on the car hood. With narrow roads lined by redbrick buildings that went up four or five stories, sounds of all kinds echoed.

One night, the echoes of Beacon Hill sounded like a city after an earthquake. I was walking back from a Sox game with a friend who was a banker. He told me of his bride, who worked for a Yellow Pages marketing company. Six months into the marriage, she had lost her job but kept it a secret, too embarrassed to tell her husband. Unemployed, each morning she dressed for work and headed out the door with briefcase in hand. Knowing that her husband would follow five minutes after she left, she'd walk the streets for fifteen minutes, then return home and watch TV for the day.

Responsible for paying the rent and now with no income, she signed up for the credit card and personal loan offers that clog mailboxes. When the landlord called saying the rent was past due, she erased the messages.

After she had been out of work for six months, debt mounting, her banker husband was called to his boss's office. "Sit down."

"Is everything OK at home?" his boss asked. "Your credit is shot. You can't work here unless you explain this."

"I don't know what to say," said the husband. "This is news to me."

In the hospital we had vast banks of clinical data stored on computer servers we could tap into; so did he. As he logged onto company's database and followed the trail of new credit card enrollments and subsequent defaults, he deciphered his new bride's tangle.

Fenway Park to Beacon Hill is a twenty-minute walk. To cross from one end of the Hill to the other takes fifteen minutes more. As we walked back from a game the Sox had lost when Toronto scored eight runs over the last two innings, he spoke of his wife and his imminent firing.

The story began outside the Rathskeller Pub in Kenmore Square. The more he talked, the more he began to perspire, beads of sweat filling his brow and then soaking his shirt. He rattled off her credit cards. There was the Save the Whales MasterCard that came with a free T-shirt. There was the Princeton Tiger Visa card that came with a coffee mug; she didn't even know where Princeton was located. There was a Save the Children Master-Card that came with a child that she supported for sixteen dollars a month.

As we reached the Beacon Hill border, he was in full rage. A hefty person who had played football in high school and college, he still weighed over 250 pounds, but most of his muscle had shifted to fat.

Like a cat jumping from hood to hood to avoid road puddles after new rain, he jumped on hood after hood in anger, slamming into fenders too.

His pounces triggered car alarms. Hearing the trail of beeping horns, seeing the succession of flashing head- and taillights, he now jumped with the deliberate intention of waking the Hill. Mercedes Benzes, BMWs, Acuras, Audis—all alarmed cars were targets. And as we walked from one end of the Hill to the other, he recounted more card names and loans as the wave of night noise grew and echoed.

The Beacon Hill drunks sleeping in doorways came to life from their alcoholic stupors. Lights went on in dark bedrooms, and tenants leaned out windows, looking right and left. That night, more than one hundred car alarms sounded. Some of the couples who lived on the Hill called the police that night and were told, "Go back to sleep. Just a little earthquake."

Hearing this explanation, couples asked each other, "We get earthquakes here?"

"I dunno?" they answered.

But the cause of the sleep-interrupted night was known only to us.

"What are you going to do?" I asked the banker.

"What could I do? I had two choices: Kill or forgive her!" he said.

Wags and I were not on call for the coming weekend. In the afternoon we ran along the Charles, looking for the TV crews filming background footage for the weather report. Finding the cameras, we sucked in our stomachs; we were now on Boston TV a fifth time. Our run over, we showered and went to the riverbank to read medical journals and the papers our seniors had given us.

That evening I went to Marblehead with one of the Cathys. Not being from New England, I was taken by the houses with fading cedar-shingle sides, six-over-six windows with blue or red gloss trim, and pitched roofs with gray slate tiles. Streets were paved with fieldstones or cobblestones. Fieldstone foundations rose a yard from the ground, gray mortar filling the cracks between the stones.

That night in Marblehead was the last time I saw this night's Cathy. Two days later she was off to Saudi Arabia to work as a travel nurse for big money, more than triple her salary in Boston. Before she left she said, "Please wait for me." But while in Saudi Arabia she met a pharmacist, whom she married.

This night was the last time I saw Mongo too. "There's a great bar I want to take you to," Cathy said, pulling me by the hand. Like the others in town, the building had faded cedar shingles and red-paint trim. We heard glass breaking as we walked up, not typical bar noise. Looking in a window, we saw a bar in full fight. Like in Western movies, bottles and glasses were being thrown, chairs lifted and tossed. Patrons were being lifted and thrown. *Is this real,* I asked myself?

Then, out of the bar doors burst Mongo. Huge, with a torso of muscle like a centaur, his shirt was torn and his back had bloody scratches.

"I know him," I yelled, now pulling Cathy by *her* hand. Mongo didn't run out of the bar; he walked slowly, like a cowboy heading off into the sunset. He walked twenty paces out the door, heading up the cobblestone road lined with black gas lamps and racks of postcards to be sold to the summer tourists.

The bar crowd exploded out the front door. Skinny kids, the thickness of one of Mongo's legs, sprinted to Mongo and pounced on his back like alley cats jumping on pork chops left on a window ledge.

Whump!

One punch from Mongo and the first kid was down, unconscious. I hadn't seen someone knocked unconscious in person before. Sure, I had seen knockouts on TV, in movies, and while watching boxing. Yet even in boxing matches, the single knockout punch is rare.

Mongo kept walking. Three skinny kids were still jumping onto his back, trying to slow him down.

Whump.

Another kid was down and unconscious.

Mongo walked twenty more feet and swung again.

Whump!

Another kid was on the ground, moaning.

Another twenty steps he walked and then faded into the harbor mist.

Four unconscious kids were now lying on the cobblestone street, each twenty feet from the other. I wondered if Mongo counted his steps between each swat.

Cathy and I were now between the four twenty-year-olds and a bar full of drunks who were watching us giving first aid to the one who still wasn't moving after Mongo's punch.

Most physicians aren't good with first aid. We work in hospitals, with medical backup everywhere. Stretchers and code carts are around every corner. A primary responder role was new for me. I stabilized the boy's neck and cleared his airway.

Then the bar drunks started giving advice. "He's having a seizure!" yelled one.

"Stick your wallet in his mouth," said another.

A pretty girl added, "Give him mouth to mouth."

Another bar patron kneeled beside me and flashed his EMT badge. "I'll take over from here, Doc," he said. I recognized him as an ambulance driver I knew from the hospital and was happy to honor his request. Looking up the street, I saw the three other kids now sitting on the cobblestones holding their heads.

When Mongo walked away, he never looked back. We never heard sirens, but an ambulance arrived with just lights flashing. The attendants scooped up the skinny kid and put him on the skinny stretcher. He was taken to a local hospital; I never learned his fate, or Mongo's.

Wags too explored a part of Massachusetts that weekend, heading off to Cape Cod, or the "Cod," as he wrongly called it. Locals call it the "Cape."

He stopped in the town of Chatham, recognizing the name from a bar we frequented. Chatham's Corner, in Faneuil Hall, had a dance club on the second floor and a bar on the first. There Wags and I watched Larry Bird steal the in-bounds pass from Isaiah Thomas when it seemed certain the Detroit Pistons were sending the Celtics packing for home in a playoff game.

"Larry Bird stole the ball! Larry Bird stole the ball!" Johnny Most, the Celtics' announcer screamed into his microphone as the bar—and Boston—erupted in cheers. With a girl whose ankle he had bandaged in the EW after she fell off her high shoes while dancing at a club on Lansdowne Street, Wags found a parking space in a lot near a packed beach. The sun of New England summers is strong, and families cover themselves with great umbrellas pushed a foot or so into the loose sand. Wags sat on the end of the beach with his date. With his hospital-white intern skin, he too rented an umbrella, jamming it into the sand.

Late in the afternoon, the salty wind blew in strong from the ocean, and Wags saw umbrellas blow out of their firm footings. When his umbrella blew down, he rolled it up. Becoming progressively redder from the beating sun, Wags prepared to leave, wondering how bad the Cape-to-Boston traffic would be.

Then Wags heard screams. He saw a huge umbrella slowly cartwheeling down the beach with the tempo of a young gymnast. Glimpsing a succession of blue, white, and silver, Wags saw the umbrella flip ten times over thirty yards.

Then he heard a man's scream and a shout: "Is there a doctor? *I need a doctor!*" the man repeated.

"I'm a doctor!" Wags yelled, jumping up from the sand.

"Come here quickly," said the man. "It's horrible! Please help!"

Vacationing from Naples, Italy, was a family of four—a black-haired wife as tan as she was thin, preteen daughters, and a husband, tall and tan. He wore a navy nylon bathing suit comprising slightly more fabric than his wife's bikini bottom. It was the kind of skimpy bathing suit that says, "You prudish descendants of the Puritans, look at me. I'm a *real* man from Europe."

He had been lying on his stomach, legs spread a bit and toes pointed out when the cartwheeling umbrella hit ground zero. *Whump!* The metal umbrella pole stuck in his rectum, stayed there for a long minute, then continued flipping down the beach until it was tackled by a teenager.

As expressive as Italian is, *no* language has the words to express your thoughts when you are awakened by an umbrella impaling your ass. The man and his family screamed, each of the four voices louder than the others.

Wags ran to the site of the impalement. The lifeguards were there with a medical kit; a glove pack was held open. "Doctor, explore the wound," said the lifeguard.

Snapping on the rubber gloves, Wags was now a beach hero. His date watched the other beachgoers staring at her lobster-red beau. She felt proud to know him.

Pulling on the navy nylon that had been pushed inside the man by the umbrella point, Wags went to work. As he applied his trade, screams of Italian blended with choruses of "Oh, my God." The impalee lay on his stomach, crying and pounding the sand with his fist. The more Wags probed, the more the crowd grew. Seagulls perched close to Wags too, flying off with the bloody gauzes Wags tossed behind him when they were saturated.

Ten-year-old girls crawled their way to the first-aid front to get a glimpse of the bloody, oozing rectum. Looking at them, Wags realized he had probed enough. He asked for more gauze and packed the wound, trying to keep the blowing sand out.

The EMTs arrived. Seeing the softball-size gauze packing of blood, sand, and tape over the man's bottom, they asked, "Doctor, rectum?"

Wags stood and smiled. "Wrecked him? Damn near killed him!" he said. The ambulance arrived to take the Italian family to Cape Cod Hospital. Following Wags's advice, the man was transported on his stomach.

Like so many of those we tended to, we never learned the fate of the vacationer. One thing we did know was that his bikini-bottom bathing suits days were over.

As the ambulance driver turned on its sirens, Wags left for his car. His date was rubbing his back saying, "I'm so proud of you. You really know your anatomy," she said with a wink.

Wags's travel timing was perfect as he pulled onto Route 6. A pediatric transport team was on the way back to Boston with a sick premature infant. Wags planted his blue Cutlass on the bumper of the ambulance and ambulance-surfed his way back home.

Monday we were back at work and Wags was sunburned and starting to peel. At the evening meal, a crowd gathered as I told my Marblehead story and Wags related his tale of the Chatham umbrella. That night we purposely spoke loudly enough so that Sputum Man and the Gypsies could hear our tales of the wacky New England weekend.

The Princess's Liver

We weren't sure where the donor liver came from, but we recognized where the princess was from. A niece of a Saudi Arabian king, at the age of sixteen she was succumbing to liver failure caused by parasitic hepatitis.

The princess arrived as I was finishing my electric block of time as a pediatric surgeon—an engaging time that made me wonder if I should change careers. But I was better suited to the open range of the EW and the wards than the gowned quarters of the OR.

The princess's operation was the first liver transplant performed at Man's Greatest Hospital. There were several patients dying of liver failure in the area, both young and old. But we did not ask why she was the first to receive a transplant.

I camped out in the hallway of the wing of the "rich and famous." Specialists of mixed ages—Gray Hairs with their short white coats, the youthful in dark suits—waited in queue for a short patient interview. Not allowed in the room, I glanced from the threshold, seeing that the princess was bright yellow. She appeared tired and weak, with Olive Oyl arms folded on her bloated stomach.

The fact that the first liver transplant was going to be on a pediatric patient was a boon for the specialty. The liver could have gone to an accomplished elderly scholar but didn't, being destined for a teenager.

After she received her transplant, I imagined she would live for years to share her wealth with those less fortunate, her obligation to us after she was given an extraordinary gift of rebirth. But perhaps, I considered, that gift from the princess and the royal family had come *before* they walked in the hospital lobby.

A teenager has about four quarts of blood. To guard against bleeding during surgery, she was typed and cross-matched for more than seventy-five pints of blood. Fresh-frozen plasma, rich with clotting factors, was brought in by the bucketful. To avoid competition for blood bank services, the laboratory, and surgeons, the first incision—like a NASA night launch—was to happen at 8:00 p.m.

OR3 was an interesting site for such a sacred procedure. OR3 was host to brilliant operations by day and, sometimes, sundry activities at night. After the surgical cases of the day were finished, anesthesiologists would sneak in to breathe the vapors from their anesthetic machines. The blue canisters of nitrous oxide provided a favorite buzz. When the hospital administration caught on to this abuse, they padlocked the gas units after the last case of the day.

Pediatric OR3 was also where a famous pediatric surgeon snuck his champion German shepherd in for emergency surgery. And it was home to the night moves of surgical residents, who would sneak in girls from the hospital or girls they met in Boston bars. Trouble would come when the engaged residents were caught in the ORs with women who weren't their fiancées. Occasionally, housekeeping personnel would catch couples having sex, flipping on the lights to embarrass them *after* they notified Security.

Perhaps to curb the house officer hanky-panky, there was a strong predilection to select surgical residents who were pious Mormons. Of the fifteen new residents admitted that year, three or four were Mormon. But they got caught engaging in OR sex too.

There were other areas in the hospital where house officer and house officer, house officer and nurse, or house officer and girlfriend bedded down. The more tired we were, the less inhibition reigned.

At the top of the tallest building of the hospital complex was a room with dark paneling and wall-to-wall pillows. The room was next to one where the page operators sat, setting off our beepers and making announcements heard throughout the complex. This room is now gone.

The page operators had their fill of us too. Medical students and mischievous interns would call requesting that Dr. Jack Daniels be paged. Hospital speakers would echo "Paging Dr. Jack Daniels. Paging Dr. Jack

Daniels." One evening, sounds of foreplay could be heard in the background of an overhead code call. Hospital security ran to the top floor, catching Dana naked with a married plastic surgeon. I wondered if she was after the implants Wags had suggested.

We each found our unique secret spot for late-night rendezvous. Mine was near the oldest part of the hospital, with walls lined with brown-and-white portraits of the physician leaders and famous scientists of years ago. On the long weekends of call, I would meet a girl from New Jersey who flew in to help make my nights pass more quickly.

Two surgical residents were once discovered around 3:00 a.m. having stand-up sex behind a free-standing poster in a main hospital hallway. The poster was toppled by an inadvertent elbow, leaving them buck naked, scrubs at their feet.

This night, however, OR3 was used for its intended purpose—it was ready for the princess's liver to be swapped in. The case started with forty personnel in the room, including three teams of surgeons and two teams of anesthesiologists. Transfusion and clotting specialists were present as well.

Standing in the back with another intern, I saw nothing, wishing the case could have been performed in the old-style operating room theaters of Thomas Eakins paintings, where students and surgeons strained at the edges of chairs for a peek at the case. We did have a venerable OR, with steps sloping up, once used for amphitheater surgery. The operations in that room, though, had ended more than seventy years ago; the hall now held an ancient mummy and a large white screen for lecture projections.

After three hours of listening to the surgeons at the table mumble to one another, their words blending with the intermittent *whoosh* of suction machines, the old liver was out. The liver was tough as shoe leather and yellow, pockmarked, and irregular.

We took turns having our photographs taken holding the decayed liver. With a three-inch space between our masks and our caps, we were indistinguishable. The person taking the photos was an anesthesiologist, who could not determine which photo went to whom. Uncollected, the photos sat in a shoe box in his office closet.

The photo shoots over, the new liver arrived, plump and maroon. We didn't learn the circumstances of the donor's demise, perhaps a car crash, a drowning, or a shooting. When the blood vessels of the liver were joined with the blood vessels of the princess, there were joyful shouts. "It's pinking up. It's making bile!"

About three o'clock in the morning, the case wrapped up. The surgical teams snapped off their gloves, tossing bloody blue gowns onto the operating room floor.

The princess went to the intensive care unit for ten days. A week later, a private jet whisked her back home. We never learned her fate, whether the liver was rejected or not or whether she lived one, ten, or even more years.

When the room emptied, OR3 was cleaned for the next day's lineup of cases. A colectomy, a cholecystectomy, and a Whipple procedure were booked. The first incision was to be made at 7:00 a.m. Later that evening, the night after the princess's liver transplant was recorded in hospital history, OR3 was silent. A welcome respite, the room was empty of surgeons wearing blue gown and blue masks.

Or so we assumed. As we completed our rounds upstairs, we heard something. So did the janitor of OR3. Peeking around the swinging OR door, ready to flip the ten-thousand-watt light switch, he looked up at a green-mirrored OR lamp. He squinted as he looked, and as he studied the reflection, he made out two sets of scrubs on the OR floor. *Should I flip the switch?* he asked himself.

Stand By Your Intern

Our support network in those hectic days didn't include the Gray Hairs. It was made up of our coresidents, with whom we shared the bond of front-line care for the sick. We quickly discovered that our ways, our beliefs of what was correct—the arrogance of youth—sometimes put us in conflict with those who taught us.

One conflict came from Honduras. Dr. Ren placed a phone call to the intensive care unit notifying us that conjoined twins had recently been born. Supposedly joined at the chest wall but with separate hearts, livers, and kidneys, this would be the slam dunk of twin separation. Like the liver transplant, this was another headline-grabbing feat to help Man's Greatest Hospital project its reputation as a world leader in medicine.

The transport team headed off to Logan Airport to await the touchdown of the Air Central America flight. The infants were to be accompanied by a physician hailed by the sending Honduran hospital as "our best doctor."

The transport of sick children to our intensive care units populated us with children of varied ages, tubes protruding from mouths, abdomens, and sides. The transport team was a mobile unit consisting of the ambulance driver and an assistant. Included too was a pediatric transport nurse and a junior or senior resident.

Responding to calls that came in on the red phone, we'd scamper over Massachusetts, New Hampshire, Maine, and Rhode Island when panicking physicians at the other end yelled, "*We need you here now!*"

We received panicked calls describing horrific states of illness. Yet after the two hours it took us to mobilize and rush our medical carts to the child's bedside, the panicking physician was usually gone. One or two nurses would be straining over the sick child, usually an infant, and greet us with warm, calm smiles.

"I'm glad you're here. Dr. Jones is sorry, but he had to go. He said you'd do a great job."

Sometimes the physician-less infants would be denim-blue, breathing-resuscitation tubes placed in the wrong spot. Other times, the children would be sitting up, healthy and playing.

"She looks a lot better now," the nurse would say.

Every transport was an adventure of unpredictability. Occasionally the transport would be canceled en route. When the turnaround squawks came over the radio, we'd turn the ambulance to a local Dunkin' Donuts drive-through window and fill the transport incubator with glazed and jelly donuts.

Some of us would get ill on transport. Stressed with dying infants requiring resuscitation in the back of a truck swerving in and out of Boston traffic, we were hit with nausea and vomiting. We developed pounding headaches, returning home appearing as ill as the child in our charge.

As we drove at high speeds, splitting highway lanes with burps of ambulance sirens, cars would line up behind us to ambulance-surf, hanging on our bumper for a quick high-speed ride. I never saw the shameful ambulance-surfers pulled over by police, yet one of the transport teams was.

Before every transport, we alerted the appropriate state police of our impending high-speed transport and route. One cold New England night, a team was charging back from a small hospital in New Hampshire with a dying infant who kept blowing holes in his lungs. Needles were stuck in his chest to decompress the locked air that limited his ventilation.

The transport ambulance was pulled over by a Crown Victoria whose red and indigo lights overtook our emergency lights and sirens. The ambulance driver explained the situation: "We're in high-speed transport of a dying infant."

"No good," said the trooper.

We hadn't notified the New Hampshire State Police that we were going to fly up and down New England highways. He glanced in the back at the infant with a chest wall that resembled a quilled porcupine.

This was a "by-the-book" trooper. He reported the team to central dispatch, ran the ambulance license plates through the computer bank, and handed the ambulance driver a speeding ticket.

The driver could have argued his unfair summons. A golden hour had already been lost at the side of the road with a moribund infant, so he stuffed the ticket into his pocket and hit the accelerator, leaving a cloud of blue rubber smoke to drift over the police cruiser. On our way back home, the ambulance kept to the speed limit. When the infant died the next day, we blamed that precious lost hour and the trooper.

The transport team for the conjoined twins from Honduras was to have an easy time of it. To the airport and back, the trip was less than ten miles. The white-and-blue Fallons ambulance pulled up to the yellow-and-green jet. Passengers deplaned, but no doctor-infant combo was seen. Jogging up the jetway, the transport resident found a young, blue-clad flight attendant who spoke more Spanish than English.

"*Los nines est aqui ayar!*"

"*No los donde esta?*" Infant abductions are rare, and the transport resident thought, *Who would scoot off with two joined babies who would be impossible to care for?*

The Honduran physician didn't stay with the babies. He walked off the jet, collar up, sunglasses on, hidden among the other passengers. We soon heard of a Spanish-speaking physician who took up practice in Chelsea who would cancel his clinics when *Telemundo* showed soccer games from Honduras.

"There, look in the last row," said the thin flight attendant, pointing at a wicker basket that was woven to the contour of the chest-to-chest infants. Pulling back the knitted wool blanket, he saw the twins, like sumo wrestlers chest-bumping and face to face with each other. Each was given the same first name, José, but they had a different "holy" middle name. One was José Angel, the other José Jesús.

"Here you go," said the flight attendant, and the basket was placed in the hands of the transport resident, and into the black hole of American health care went the Josés—no parents, no physician.

The transport resident was a sharp fellow—a Preparation H. Stethoscope in ears, listening to the infants above the jet motors, he knew there weren't separate hearts. The infants were a mixture of yellow and blue, liver disease and heart disease.

The transport was now in earnest; lights and sirens on, the ambulance left the Logan Airport runway. The children would soon be in the neonatal intensive care unit, the NICU.

We see many strange things in medicine, weird things that infants are born with and peculiar things that people do to themselves and others. When these weird things happen, the voyeur in us takes over. "I was in the neighborhood. Can I see?" was asked in repetition. And the NICU was now full of doctors, nurses, and administrators, rubber necks stretched for a peek. This was the same group that showed up to look at Maggot Man and his wiggling brain scan. They snuck in to see the teenage boy who fit a two-liter soda bottle up his rectum. They snuck in to see the child who had been stabbed in his pituitary gland with a curtain rod. But conjoined twins? This medical act wasn't to be missed.

One voyeur even walked off with the special wicker basket, which she later used as a bed for her spaniels.

I was in the NICU when the babies arrived. The surgeons, the miracle workers to be, were going to make two babies from a clump of hearts, livers, and bowel. Anxious, they paced in their OR greens, waiting to examine the twins with the holy names.

The physicians in Honduras must have been confused. José and José had a single malformed heart with five chambers that didn't pump well. Looking at the chest X-ray, the radiologist blurted, "A blind kangaroo at night could see that there is only one heart and one liver." The surgeons left the NICU muttering weird acronyms in their discontent.

Voyeuristic interest over, José and José were left face to face on a raised warming table. White spotlights shined on the yellow-and-blue infants, whose heads curved back like commas. The cardiologist arrived, hoping to mentally dissect the heart anatomy.

His bald top was ringed with red, wiry hair resembling Bozo the Clown, who had scared more children in his TV lifetime than he amused. One of the NICU nurses, who grew up in Medford, appeared on the Bozo show when she was six years old. Twenty years later, she would have disturbing flashbacks of the crimson-headed clown when the cardiologist arrived.

"José has a duct-dependent lesion!" Bozo the Cardiologist said. "We must give him prostaglandins!"

The duct is a small vessel that joins the aorta with the pulmonary artery. Normally this structure closes soon after birth. In some babies with misplumbed hearts, keeping the vessel open preserves critical blood flow.

The cardiologist charged at the Josés with a syringe full of prostaglandins. He knew that prostaglandins dilated blood vessels. We knew that they could also stop breathing.

"Stop!" yelled my senior, a Practical Senior with great judgment, calm in harried settings. We were too late. First José Angel stopped breathing, then José Jesús. The mixture of yellow and blue was now yellow and purple. The top of the cardiologist's head now matched his hair, making him look like a bald man who forgot his hat at Ipswich Beach in mid-August.

But the Practical Senior was smooth. I grabbed the Josés, spinning José Angel down as the senior slid the endotracheal tube into the windpipe. We then flipped the Josés. Back on the table, José Jesús was intubated next. Face to face, breathing tubes in place, they looked like tango dancers. The red-faced cardiologist slithered out of the NICU.

Our quick actions got them breathing again, but the Josés died later that evening. The mother and father, living in a remote Honduran village, and the Honduran escort physician were unaware of the night's events. We imagined the parents looking to the sky for a divine sign. I imagined two small stars arcing over their small village.

The word of the double-flip intubation spread department to department and was the talk of the evening meal for a week. The cardiologist was summoned to the Chair to explain his actions. As with most senior staff blunders, his actions were considered "appropriate" in public. Through back channels, though, we heard that he'd been taken to the woodshed and admonished for his actions.

Back-channel communications also were sent by the Chair to thank us for our heroism. Such commendations were rare. We were expected to perform miracles; lifesaving was just another day at the office.

Another showing of team collective, us-versus-them, happened later in my first year. The ward team was big: one senior resident, two junior residents, and two interns.

My co-intern had attended Princeton as an undergraduate before going to Johns Hopkins Medical School, where he was tortured with exams. We were paired together most of the year, working well together. He knew when to expect children to talk; I knew when to expect their teeth to erupt. He knew each of the monuments at Yankee Stadium; I knew the retired numbers that hung at Fenway.

On the wards was a special room for evaluating infants with near sudden infant death syndrome (SIDS), a condition championed by one of the attendings but later roundly disproved. He developed special monitoring devices to detect respiratory movement, and these devices were worn on children's bellies coast to coast. When the respiratory tracings looked suspicious, the local physician would contact the SIDs attending, who would recommend further evaluation.

Families would fly into Logan Airport, soon to be taxied to Mass General to have their child admitted for daylong studies.

Taking the history, we heard, "Johnny stopped breathing for *five* minutes."

"What did you do?" we'd ask.

"Well, we only noticed it for the last ten seconds, and we shook him then."

"How do you know he stopped breathing for five minutes?" we'd ask.

"We just do!" they'd answer.

"What was Johnny wearing?" we'd ask.

"He was wearing a blue Snuggie under the blanket that his Aunt Tippy knitted for him."

"Were the lights on?" we asked next.

"Doctor, what baby sleeps with a light on?" the parents would say.

We got the point about what was ahead. Occasionally the home-printed monitor tracings were presented, showing that the child had stopped breathing for twenty, forty, or sixty seconds. But these devices were as accurate as weather forecasts.

In one case, the mother reported having had three children die from SIDS. We were told by the attending, "This is what it's all about. Saving lives! We need to help this mother, who has lost three sons." The trumpets blaring like a charge by General Patton.

Ten years later, while watching *60 Minutes,* we learned that this mother had been smothering her children. What was considered a medical mystery was medically assisted murder. The blazing diagnosis of familial SIDS was debunked.

There were other times when *60 Minutes* would show up at Man's Greatest Hospital's threshold. Ed Bradley or Morley Safer would appear, trailed by a string of cameramen tethered to tightly curled black cords connected to battery packs on belts. The voyeur pack that appeared with the arrival of the twin Josés followed the TV crews from a safe distance, eager to see who would be the victim of the interview pounce.

The hospital media relations office ducked into bomb shelters during these investigative inquiries. There were no press releases. Administrators gone, physicians were on their own to wish for Valium, trying to think clearly under the white lights, their tongues as stiff as clogs.

I imagined being asked, "Doctor, now tell me about the fifteen children in Somerville born with a wing in place of a foot. Doctor, did it ever occur to you that there could have been a serious connection?"

The responses were always the same.

"Certainly, we considered the possibility of association after the fifteenth child was born with a wing instead of a foot. When this occurred, we reported it to the state."

The three-quarter portrait camera shot of the doctor would fade away, to be replaced by an image of the abandoned Schrafft's chocolate factory in Charlestown showing teens sneaking in to snack on waste chocolate.

"Doctor, did it ever occur to you that the mothers of these children came from the same area, and *all* had eaten expired chocolate when they were young?"

"Well, no," the physician would say.

And that was the reporter's winning "gotcha" shot.

As interns, it was our task to interview nervous parents and grandparents resolute in the belief that their child had died and miraculously returned to life. They would hold monitor tracings, saying, "We want our child's records available to help others." They thought their child's recovery held the solution to the Rubik's Cube of a real condition.

We knew better. Day after day we admitted infants, interviewed parents, and discharged infants from the monitoring rooms, finding pathology only in the parents and the SIDS-championing attending. That said, we became part of the machine that sent families home with SIDS monitors. Silver leads were glued to the babies, making them look like mini-astronauts with biotelemetry packs.

"This is wrong!" said the junior residents ready to take a stand. "These children are not sick. This is crap! There's no evidence this nonsense works."

This defiance was welcomed by our senior, who was the Avant-garde Senior. If there was a conventional way to do things, he took the opposite path. If teenage kids with cancer were getting chemotherapy, instead of prescribing the antinausea medications the rest of us ordered, he took them to the outside deck and smoked pot with them. The kids would giggle and burp up smoke during their treatments. "They never vomit," he bragged.

"Doctor, why do your patients always do so well?" asked one mother. "You must be a *very* special doctor!"

He was indeed special. I remember the same senior arrogantly admonishing a parent who thought she had just poisoned her febrile three-year-old by administering Tylenol. On call for forty-eight hours, he was unaware of the wacko in Chicago who had laced Tylenol with arsenic, killing people with colds and other minor ailments across the United States.

Not being in tune with the news wasn't unique for us. There wasn't time to read the *New York Times* or the *Boston Globe*, and on days off we slept through the TV news.

The senior walked the mother over to the psychiatric unit for evaluation of her bizarre ideation. One hour later, she returned madder than a whacked beehive, waving a front-page headline about the Chicago poisonings for him to read. He still didn't give a damn.

Nestled in the SIDS observation room, two out-of-state infants were in cribs separated by an aisle barely wide enough to allow a thin nurse to pass. Monitoring for potential respiratory arrest, electrodes were placed on the infants' abdomens; heart rates and respiratory patterns were assessed continuously.

"We're glad to report that all looks well," said the attending. "But to be safe, we'd like your child to go home with a monitor to use until she's ten years old. And yes, she can wear it playing soccer." Out the door the family went, new monitor in hand.

The revolving door continued. Two hours later a new baby arrived. The junior residents now had a plan. In earnest, they told the attending they believed the infants needed more thorough evaluations than were routinely taking place. As a baby was set to move out and another to rotate in, they would notice formula in the baby's mouth after a feed.

"Could this be urinary reflux? Let's consult urology. We don't want the kidneys to fail."

Two days would pass before urology recommendations and testing followed, with no problems found.

After this was done, they would notice that the baby twitched. Pediatric Neurology would be consulted and asked to weigh in about the likelihood of a seizure disorder. Electrodes would be gooped to the head to monitor brainwave activity for twenty-four hours. The formal EEG report added another two days of waiting.

With the infant cleared by the urologist and neurologist, the junior residents would notice a heart murmur. The pediatric cardiologist consult is always the same. "It's not the heart," the heart specialists would say. Even if it was not the heart, another two days got tacked on.

The strategy worked. Two days of hospitalization were stretched to eight-plus. "The SIDS beds are blocked!" the junior residents cheered.

Children waiting to fly in for evaluation now circled at home, waiting for admission. Like farmers in France who close roads in protest of low grain prices, this was the perfect strategy. Resident against attending, we stood tall.

They say that all good things must come to an end, and the end came abruptly one morning. We were rounding as a team, recounting the events and lab tests of yesterday, formulating treatment plans. The room where we met for rounds had a long, dark wood table running down the middle. Dark wood walls with nick marks bordered the room. The bookcases were stuffed with dusty, leather-bound texts and journals that hadn't been touched in decades. Interrupting our quick pace of the morning, our Chair, Dr. Ren, walked in. His face was red, and he was breathing fast.

From the height of his shoulder, he slammed a navy plastic loose-leaf hospital chart on the table. "Do I have your attention?"

The slammed chart was that of a two-month-old apnea patient kept for ten days—our new record for resident-versus-attending.

Nostrils flaring, he said, "You get your ducks in row and get this child home!" Then he left.

Dr. Ren was a wonderful man who felt incredible paternalism toward us, and we know it pained him to reprimand a house officer. But the limit of resident-versus-attending had passed tolerance, and he had to restore the proper order to our medical universe. The child was discharged a few hours later with a new SIDS monitor, and another infant rotated in to fill the vacated bed.

While our Chair was publically gruff with us, the SIDS attending was privately told to "get your ducks in a row" too. Here I saw the public-private dichotomy of discipline—the public challenge to those in training, the private rebuke to those on staff—and I saw the equity of rebuke. Most important, I saw the reflection of lofty standards of excellence applied to all.

Girls from Maine

Not long after moving to Boston, I learned that girls from New England were different from those where I came from. The stoicism and independence I came to recognize were a refreshing respite from the excessive emotion of girls from New York and New Jersey. When they spoke they said "No, Suh," or "Yes, Suh," dropping *R*'s for "ahs." Their *O*'s were longer and softer too.

Not intentionally, Wags and I had parallel rendezvous with girls from Maine, girls even more stoic and harder to crack than the Boston girls. Perhaps rooted in the ethic of the generations who logged, fished, and hauled "lobstahs," these ladies were different. Perhaps their reserved, unhurried ways came from waiting for the spring thaw that followed the rest of New England. During graduations in May and June, they looked at heaps of snow in parking lot borders as processions of graduates listened to long-winded speeches. Perhaps it was because their fathers were "Princes of Maine—Kings of New England," as John Irving proclaimed.

Wags met his girl from Maine at Faneuil Hall. I was introduced to mine by a medical school friend.

Sitting alone on a stool at Chatham's Corner, Wags engaged a pretty girl with long brown hair in polite banter. She had gone to a community college north of Portland. Tired of small-town life, she hopped a bus for Boston, planning to look for work as a secretary.

She rented a cheap apartment in Cambridge that she paid for with the tips she saved from her work as a waitress. Not being from Boston, she had true infatuation and admiration for young MDs.

My girl from Maine graduated from one of those small wood-building schools—the schoolhouse image you see on postcards. In high school she had been told she wasn't college material. Thus she was enrolled at a community college. After excelling, she transferred to one of Maine's great liberal arts schools, Colby College, with a full scholarship. Smart and classy, she reminded me of a young Mia Farrow with her looks and patient ways.

Familiar with girls who let their emotions fly, reading this girl from Maine was hard. Dates consisted of concerts, dinners, and pizza in Boston's Italian North End. There were no Red Sox games. I was enamored by her understated charm, measured speech, quick wit, and New England rationality. She could stand on her own, no need for a male crutch.

She worked for a college that gave her a comfortable apartment in Back Bay. Five floors up, her roof deck caught a magnificent view of the Charles, which sparkled at sunset.

The city from above looked nothing like the world of the streets below. The roof decks in Boston weren't high—five or six stories above the streets at most. When fireworks were shot from the Hatch Shell on the Fourth of July and Labor Day, the tops of brownstones and Federal-style redbrick buildings were jammed with cup-holding students and young adults. With each bright explosion, the city rooftops roared together.

From her roof deck, I could see the neon CITGO sign of Kenmore Square near Fenway Park blink white and red. White-and-black nighthawks darted along the evening sky, feeding on mosquitoes and moths. Occasionally the night moths invaded games at Fenway, with play stopping until they passed. Bats, not the baseball kind, were seen too, though rarely.

We didn't date our girls from Maine long. Wags last date with his girl was with a group of four couples. One couple included the ambitious Cardiac Kid, whose pants I had filled with ultrasound paste, and his girlfriend. She was loud, pretty, and blond. They later married. The priest at their wedding said to the congregation, "On their first date they went to church. How nice!" Our pew exploded in unison, "That's because they woke up together on Sunday morning saying, 'What do you want to do now?'"

I was with my girl from Maine. Another of our friends, the Checkmark Resident, was with a nurse from the pediatric intensive care unit whom he would later marry. Wags brought his girl from Maine, newly in town to pound a typewriter, take dictation, and run errands.

At the evening's start, it was obvious that she was uncomfortable with us, out of sorts with the "you can't believe this" stories we told about the hospital happening of the week. We did our best to make her feel welcome, and after two drinks her stiff shoulders settled and she smiled. She traded seats with me to swap Down East stories with my girl from Maine, but the small talk was small.

The Scotch and Sirloin was on the top floor of a ten-story building in the North End beside the highway that cut Boston in half. After a few drinks had been served, I smiled at the bright lights of the city and suggested that we head to the salad bar.

Wags excused himself and headed to the men's room, saying, "Y'all just go on ahead. I'll catch up with you."

We slid our plates along the steel countertop. I was next to both girls from Maine as I saw Wags walking in our direction.

I next heard shouts from the Cardiac Kid's girlfriend, who was pointing and laughing in disbelief.

"*Ohhhhh, my God! His penis is out!*" she yelled.

Such a pronouncement will silence a rally at Fenway Park. In a small, classy restaurant, it froze us as though gassed with a paralytic. The heads of the other diners swung in unison—forks, glasses, and words frozen in midair.

Wags, in a hurry to join his girl from Maine, had forgotten to perform the most obvious unconscious act each male does when backing away from a urinal.

Sure that he had fixed his hair in the mirror before leaving the men's room, I turned to the girls from Maine and said, "Doesn't his hair look great?" But there were no laughs.

There we stood at the salad bar, the other diners in wide-eyed attention, looking at Wags's penis dangling near the steel countertop. Recognizing the problem after one of the other surgeons caught his eye and pointed, too embarrassed to be embarrassed, Wags laughed, tucked himself in, and began to fill his salad plate. Ten minutes later he was drinking from a carafe of white wine, joking with the rest of us.

For the remainder of the evening, Wags's girl from Maine could neither look at nor talk to Wags or us. She wasn't wise to the art of "beeping" herself out of uncomfortable spots, choosing to remain Maine-style stoic.

Each day in medicine we see what's normally hidden to lay people: Breasts, penises, and the low-hanging scrotums of aging veterans are daily sights. Care of the nude is a routine business, and the sicker you are, the more modesty fades. But to a girl from Maine, in town to work behind a desk, such a sight in a fine restaurant was no less than bizarre.

We finished our dessert-less meal; we didn't have coffee, nor did we mention Wags's faux pas. We went to the Checkmark Resident's Beacon Hill apartment for a nightcap, to talk and laugh more. We awaited Wags's arrival, which we expected would be late and alone. It was.

As most natives know, a common and dreaded vehicle in Boston is the tow truck—not surprising for a city where parking spaces are as rare as Yankee fans. And the tow truck is as despised as the Yankee fan. We heard that kickbacks and bribes happened among the towing companies that fought for haul-away rights, as each tow put seventy-five dollars in the operator's pocket.

Wags and I were fodder for these hucksters. If you parked your car over a curb on Beacon Hill, off your car went. If you parked within nine feet of a fire hydrant, you could say good-bye to your car. Park at 5:55 p.m. on Cambridge Street, five minutes too soon, and your car was gone.

So seldom did we drive, we often didn't know our car had been brought to a tow lot. One spring, having last used Wags's Cutlass in February, Wags and I were off to buy Sox tickets. Not seeing the Cutlass where he had last parked it, we knew he'd been towed again, eventually learning the car was in Charlestown. I drove my white Fiat to the lot with Wags, only to learn that the lot wasn't staffed on mid-Sunday afternoons. An unusual impound, the cars were penned in by telephone poles arranged end to end. We log-rolled a pole away from the Cutlass, and Wags drove away, avoiding four hundred dollars in impound and towing fees.

Another time, a Cathy parked my Fiat on Cambridge Avenue five minutes before the allowed parking time of 6:00 p.m. I learned that the vehicle was in "Southie," so we taxied to South Boston where hundreds of "cahs" were secured by chain-link fences and razor wire; there would be no quick getaway this time.

I next learned that they only took cash. Since I lived paycheck to paycheck, money in my pocket was never one of my strong suits. Stuck in Southie without cab fare home and no banks in the area, I lost my temper.

"How could you park the car there? What are we going to do now?"

An earshot away, a white-haired man in his late forties with a girl about thirty walked over.

"How much do you need?" he said.

"Seventy-five dollars," I sighed.

Reaching into his shirt pocket, he pulled out a three-inch wad of hundred-dollar bills.

"Here," he said. A hundred bucks was mine, and we were out of there.

I took his address and sent him the money he loaned me along with a note of appreciation. At first he was reluctant to give his name, making us think that he was connected. He wasn't. He was just a successful person who had parked his Porsche in the wrong spot.

Before dinner, Wags and his girl from Maine had parked the Cutlass under a green metal stanchion that supported Interstate 93. Two blocks from Boston Garden, there were no signs prohibiting parking, but no other cars were there. After dinner, following a silent elevator ride to the street and a chilly, short walk, they discovered that the blue Cutlass was gone. Like me, Wags never had a penny in his pocket.

The girl from Maine reached into her pocket of tip money and paid for the cab to the South End. No rich benefactor in sight, she paid one hundred dollars and the car was released.

"Please let me get home soon," she prayed.

Not planning to drive far that evening, Wags arrived at the girl's apartment with his fuel tank empty. She now ponied up money for gas, fearing she might again be stranded along Interstate 93, trapped in a night that would never end.

Ninety minutes later we heard Wags bounding up the steps. He was alone.

"You're not gonna believe what happened," he said.

"Yes we can!" we said as a group.

He told us how it came to be that this girl from Maine, who had come to Boston with no more than three hundred dollars in her wallet, was now considerably poorer because of him.

"I'll pay her back," he said.

But his phone calls to her were never returned.

Six months later, the Checkmark Resident was having a beer at Faneuil Hall when he was tapped on the shoulder by a girl with short brown hair.

"Hey, remember me? Your friend owes me $150," she said.

No expletives spoken, plain like her state, she spoke her deserved request softly. They found a bank machine, and the debt was settled.

The Checkmark Resident, embarrassed for his friend, walked away from her as fast as she had walked up to him.

"She looked great," he told Wags. Her hair was shorter, she had shed her clunky shoes, and she now had a tight above-the-knee skirt like a Boston Proper girl.

When he finally pulled up in front of her doorway at night's end, Wags's girl from Maine had run away from him as fast as a track star. My girl from Maine, though, slowly flickered out. More familiar with girls who wore their emotions on their sleeves, I tried to crack her New England reserve, but she was too hard for this house officer to read. I knew all along that she was waiting for me to calm and mature. Perhaps she was right, but that would take years. When her phone messages became mixed with the frenetic calls of the Cathys, I returned the Cathys' calls. Outmuscled by the girls of New York, I let her fade away.

Now whenever I read of Mia Farrow, her successes and problems, I think of my girl from Maine. I wonder about her successes and pains in the ensuing years, wanting to tell her that, a decade later, I could now appreciate her Maine ways.

Taking the Wrong Thing

At 10:00 p.m. Wags answered a call from Nikki at the triage desk. "Shotgun Man" was back and breathing fast. Fifty hospitalizations after the initial blast, he was in a recurrent Sisyphean hell of facial, head, and neck repairs. This was the start of our lessons of self-inflicted sadness.

Shotgun Man was about forty years old. When he was thirty-five, he put his toe in a shotgun trigger. Depressing the trigger, he arched the barrel of the gun back. Instead of sending shrapnel under his chin to bring the death that he wanted, the blast sent steel pellets forward of a death shot. He blew off his chin, the front of his tongue, and most of his face.

The hundred or more surgeons, anesthetists, nurses, residents, and medical students who cared for this man over the years knew little of Shotgun Man. Why did he pull the trigger? What was the state of his current depression? No one asked. Dealing with the consequences of the mangling blast, each admission was similar—continue facial reconstruction; continue to undo what Shotgun Man did to himself.

Unsure why Shotgun Man was in the EW now, Wags tried to get information from Nikki, without luck. Wags and Nikki had history.

Nikki was five foot six inches tall, thin, and tan, even in mid-February. She looked like a stretched version of Angie Dickinson. As stiff as she was tan, behind her back she was called Nurse Ratched, the stern nurse in *One Flew over the Cuckoo's Nest.*

She was more than ten years older than we, and she preyed on the surgical residents. Earlier in the year she tried to spin her web around Wags, offering to help him with blood draws that were not that tough. Just after Nikki's shift began one October night, Wags and Nikki bent over the mid-arm of an elderly man, one whose veins rolled under loose, elastic, waxy skin. She bent in a way that made her breasts pop out of the top of her white tapered uniform, and Wags did stare.

Old-school, Nikki wore white nurse's stockings and white shoes. She wore a uniform like those seen in the stern black-and-white photographs randomly placed on walls throughout the hospital. She liked the tall, youthful interns. Wags hit her mark on three counts: youth, height, and naiveté. She was also intrigued by his impressive salad bar revelation, which was no longer a secret.

Assisting Wags in a blood draw, she put her shoulders together even more than before, and Wags stared even more. Wags hit a rolling vein and drew back on a twenty cc syringe, aiming to fill it for the ordered tests. Wags pulled back on the syringe plunger while Nikki was to his left holding the wrinkled arm. She was looking at the arm and syringe as Wags noticed one nipple, now fully exposed.

Then Nikki shouted, "Oh, my God."

Wags over-pulled the plunger, and it came back out of the syringe with a pop. Nikki hopped back, twenty ccs of blood now running down her right leg to puddle in her shoe. Red on white nylons, red into white tie shoe, Nikki looked like a Jackson Pollock painting.

Usually one can spot the degree of nursing fury by the shade of facial redness. But Nikki's face was wooden, so Wags missed the cue about how furious she was. He continued to speak to her as he redrew the blood sample, until he felt the heat coming from Nikki's over-tanned, blush-hiding face.

One of my senior residents used to say, "Nurses are like elephants. They never forget." Wags learned how true this adage was. From that moment on, Nikki never made work comfortable for him. Wags had to hunt for charts. He drew blood alone. He had to call report to the floors. And now he was on his own with Shotgun Man.

Trying to get a history from Shotgun Man was impossible. With his scarred mouth opening and lack of tongue, one had to guess at the guttural sounds. With each trip to the hospital, Shotgun Man's brother, who worked in the Charlestown Navy Yard, would drop him off at the emergency entrance. Leaving his van idling, he'd say a few curt words to the charge nurse and then drive off.

Shotgun Man was now breathing fast and drooling. Wags started an IV and drew blood alone, looking for revealing clues. He ordered an X-ray of the head, neck, and chest; all the while, Nikki was doing these things for the other tall residents she was eying that night.

I was on call in the pediatric side of the EW that evening. A C-Med radio call came over the EW nursing station speaker. They were en route with a sixteen-year-old boy who had jumped off the Tobin Bridge. Many cities have elegant bridges that span waterways and are famous landmarks shown on postcards. But the Tobin Bridge is not art. Linking Boston to Chelsea, the bridge is a utilitarian web of green girders that looks like a solution to a problem given to sophomore engineering students.

At mid-span, the bridge is five hundred feet above Boston Harbor. At full jump, hitting the water is like landing on concrete.

The boy en route had hoped he would later be found washed up on the seawall at Logan Airport. But, plop, he had landed in the water and wasn't dead. His right leg ached, not much else. What was he to do now, alive and bobbing in oily water? He bobbed there for a while, hoping he'd drown. He continued to bob, hoping for a large vessel or an oil tanker to plow him under, but there was no large-vessel traffic that night.

I'm not sure how he lived after he jumped. Perhaps he hit the wake of a boat that broke the surface, softening his landing. Alive, he swam a mile to the shore of East Boston, climbed out of the water, and pounded on the back door of a woman's home. Fearing a burglar, she called the police as she reached for her dead husband's shotgun, pumping a round into the chamber. Hearing the shotgun pump, the boy froze, yelling, "Don't shoot me. Please don't shoot me. I need help!"

Like going over Niagara Falls in a barrel, more people die than live after a plunge into the dark waters of Boston Harbor. He was a surviving soul and now was on his way to the EW by ambulance.

The conclusion to a city-mesmerizing murder took place on the same green bridge. A greedy fur store manager from a Boston suburb took out an insurance policy on his pregnant wife for more than six hundred thousand dollars. Claiming to have gotten lost while returning from childbirth classes in a poor part of Boston, he said he and his wife had been shot by a black man when he stopped at a traffic light. The wife and unborn child died, but he survived to read poetry at their tearful funerals. He later confessed to the murders in a note he left on the top of that green bridge before jumping to his death; he washed up in East Boston.

I was told that some at Mass General knew he was guilty before the jump. His brother, hospitalized and delirious with an infection that closed his throat three weeks before the jump, shouted "He did it!" He did it!"

"He did what?" the nurses at his hospital bed would ask.

"My brother did it! My brother did it!" he'd yell.

The higher his fever and pain went, the more he talked, and the confession followed. Taking their turns behind the closed curtain that hid the brother's bed, the nurses asked their questions.

"Where'd ya get the gun?"

"Where's the gun now?"

"Why'd ya brotha do it?"

As the confession went on, they called the police. I imagined that the charge nurse, who scribbled the notes of the confession on the hospital anesthesia flow sheets, spoke first, surrounded by the younger nurses. She would begin, "First he said, 'My brother did it.' Then he said he worked at a hardware store. Then he said he bought a lunch box at Grossman's to put the gun in. Then he said he washed his car so there would be no fingerprints. Then he said he polished the bullets." I could imagine the detective turning pages of his flip pad taking notes, saying "I see" after each spoken sentence before asking, "Can you please slow down?"

I could see the charge nurse interrupted by the others: "No, this is what he said," or "Tell him that he said this," or "Tell the detective what he said when his temperature was *really* high." They each wanted the part of the confession they heard to be the most important.

A group of bouncing nurses hell-bent on solving the crime of the decade in Boston; it was their duty. They needed to take a stand for a young pregnant woman shot and killed by her husband.

Not long after, the *Boston Globe* reported inconsistencies in the police investigation, which had falsely pegged a black drug dealer from Roxbury as the culprit. "Anonymous sources disclose there is new evidence implicating the husband in his wife's murder." The nurses of the unit wondered if a member of the community of confession was dating the reporter. Perhaps the detective leaked their confession to pressure the killer.

Three weeks later, a news report flashed midday on the TV screen in the unit. TVs were always on, watched as much by the staff as by the patients. A reporter was standing on the windy Tobin Bridge roadway holding a microphone. As he spoke, he held his shifting hairpiece in place with his non-microphone hand. The wind blowing into the microphone created annoying background noise, obscuring his words.

The reporter began, "I am standing on the Tobin Bridge to announce the conclusion to one of this city's most horrific crimes."

The camera rotated to the right and showed the suspect's green car. A witness came over, a toll collector.

"Please tell us what you saw," said the reporter.

Wiping his nose, the toll collector spoke, "I saw this guy get out his cah. He ran over to the rail and jumped."

"And there you have it," said the reporter.

The community of confession stood in silence. Justice complete, they went back to hanging IV drips, giving medications, and suctioning endotracheal tubes.

Wags and I met in the main part of the EW discussing my jumper. After his splashdown followed by a mile swim in cold water of the night, the teen was complaining of pain in his chest and right leg. Examining the teen, Wags said, "He has decreased breath sounds over the right lung base. He's tender under his right ribs too." Wags said to X-ray the chest, the abdomen, the pelvis, and the extremities.

As he inspected my patient, I looked at Shotgun Man in his watch. I said, "Wags, I just looked at your guy. I noticed fresh ulcers on his mouth. I touched them. They're soapy."

My kid's X-rays came back. There was air outside the lungs and around the heart. The right femur was fractured. The hematocrit had dropped from 42 percent to 30. He was bleeding into his thigh and likely into his abdomen.

When brought to the EW by ambulance, he was accompanied by a woman who wasn't his mother. She was a family friend, about fifty-five years old, who lived next to the home where the boy climbed out of the muck and ooze of Boston Harbor. His mother wasn't there; neither was his father or his grandparents. The neighbor explained how Tommy lived alone at home. His father had left long ago. His mother was an alcoholic who worked in a taproom in Chelsea.

The night of his jump, she wasn't there when he needed to talk about the rotten events of the recent days, events that had become too unbearable for him to deal with. This kind neighbor would invite him to dinner in her home, sending him home with food each time. She'd do his laundry from time to time too. This night, although she wasn't, we considered her his mother.

Needing emergency surgery, with his biological mother nowhere to be found, he was wheeled to the OR holding the neighbor's hand. When the operation was over five hours later, she sat alone in the surgery waiting room awaiting the boy's return.

When the boy opened his eyes, she said, "Tommy, I called your Ma. I told her that you ah okay. She said that she'll be right ovah." Tommy knew that was a lie.

Tommy's mother appeared three days later. She was told that Tommy had torn his esophagus, lacerated his liver, and had a pneumothorax along with a fractured femur. All she said was, "That boy ain't normal in the head." Tommy looked away, thinking about the big green bridge.

While Tommy was thinking about jumping again, Shotgun Man was several steps ahead in his death quest. Years had passed since he'd pulled the trigger, and even Shotgun Man didn't know why he'd shot the gun. This time, though, he remembered what he'd done but was saddled with his inability to tell us.

The soaping lesions in his mouth became more pronounced and grew. I was proud that Wags continued to examine him. Too often in medicine, the temptation is strong to turn away from the disfigured. Wags pulled on Shotgun Man's cheeks, which had been reconstructed from gluteal tissue and gave him a round face. Zigzag scars randomly crossed his face. There in the corner of his mouth, Wags saw the evidence of a lye burn.

Shotgun Man's brother couldn't imagine how he had drunk a jug of liquid drain cleaner. Neither could we.

That night, Shotgun Man went to the OR to have his esophagus washed and debrided. Yet with lye burns, the outcome is never good—the human body has evolved to fight acid, not base solutions like lye.

After his procedure Shotgun Man spent weeks on the surgical wards, where Wags and the others waited for his esophagus to sclerose, becoming a thick, nonfunctional tube. Shotgun Man now needed to be tube-fed, first through a tube that went from his mouth to stomach, then from a catheter—a G-tube—that went directly into his stomach from the outside.

While we waited for Shotgun Man's esophagus to scar, we heard that he had been put in a room with "Lye Man." Lye Man was sixty years old, a former banker who had been caught embezzling. We never learned how much he took. The family said, "Not much."

One week before he was to go to trial, he reportedly wrote a note atoning for his actions. He said he had too much pride and too little strength for a public trial.

He gulped cupful after cupful of drain cleaner. He was found at home by one of his daughters. The burns were so severe that his esophagus fused on the spot, as did his upper airway. He was condemned to a life on a ventilator, fed with a G-tube, the red rubber catheter protruding from an oozing spot above his stomach. He had no sense of taste. He had no smell either, because the inside of his nose had been burned away by the caustic vapors.

Recuperating from his surgeries, Lye Man tried to kill himself repeatedly. He disconnected his IV line, trying to get air to enter his veins, but that didn't work. He disconnected his respirator, but that set off alarms and he got reconnected.

He learned to disconnect the respirator and plug the end of the tube to mimic the natural resistance of breathing. One day a nursing student walked by and saw his purple face. She discovered his finger at the end of the ventilator and reconnected it, the death that he wished for blocked by watchful eyes.

Eventually he was put into perpetual four-extremity restraints. Without smell, without taste, with no ability to sense the air he was breathing in, he now lost the ability to move willfully.

Lye Man now had a new roommate, Shotgun Man. And when Shotgun Man looked to his left at Lye Man, he saw the reflection of his new fate. How horrible, we thought, knowing it was our sworn obligation to keep these souls alive at all costs. And when the surgeons walked their room on morning rounds, the new roommates looked at them in unison, casting sad glances that asked for the true mercy that no one bound by the Hippocratic Oath could deliver.

Mummification

After a while, the novelty of writing orders, and having a paycheck for the first time, began to fade. With the daily grind and exhaustion of nights on your feet, boredom overcomes intellectual curiosity. Yet out of this drudgery laced with tiredness, wonderful ideas sprang from the REM (rapid eye movement) sleep that we lapsed into whenever we stopped moving.

Holding a wrist of a right-angled arm that had been hinged after a break above the elbow, Wags was asleep on his feet during an orthopedics, or "ortho," case. The ortho-tech was wrapping the arm with soft white cotton, then a layer of gauze, then a layer of wet plaster.

The last layer was the most valuable, "the money roll," as it was the layer seen and signed. If it wasn't perfect, it reflected poorly on the surgeon, no matter how complex and intricate the reconstruction. Applying the money roll, there could be no bubbles or bumps in the wet plaster. The smoothness of the last coat conferred seamless perfection. During medical school, we practiced our money roll on many things. I even plastered the torso of a roommate's pit bull terrier in a cast that was polished bone smooth.

As Wags held the wrinkled arm, dozing in and out of standing REM sleep, a brilliant thought hit him. Wags wasn't alone in REM-conceived mischievousness. The more sleep deprived, the more we REMed; the sleep deprivation triggering REM-rebound, compressing the dreams of a full night into a minute or two.

Sleep deprived, residents would jump while sitting in lectures when REM dreams had them falling off a ledge. House officers had panic attacks, dreaming they had a test the next day they had not prepared for. Young physicians would yell phrases in the middle of lectures, usually a word or two of a halting command.

This time Wags yelled, "Mummy," standing on his feet with his top eyelids touching the top of his scrub mask.

"Mummy?" the ortho-tech repeated.

Wags's eyes opened. "Mummy. Yes, I was thinking of the mummy," he said. What he didn't say was that he had had a flash dream of the hospital mummy lodging in our apartment, making friends and dates awestruck and jealous. We never knew much about the hospital mummy, Padihershef, which stood bound at attention in Mass General's most revered lecture hall. From the twenty-second Egyptian dynasty, more than twenty-five hundred years ago, he stood in a glass case covered with dust, his buntings of faded, hole-punched canvas. Day after day, medical students, house officers, and the Gray Hairs walked past him without a glance.

True or not, we heard that he had been acquired by a Harvard physician to help raise funds for Mass General Hospital and was sent on tour across the country to bring in money, a coin at a time. The mummy had found its home in the hospital amphitheater more than two hundred years ago, where it became witness to decades of lectures from those both young and esteemed, from professors and Nobel Prize winners too. And over these decades, the mummy saw the evolution of medicine from alchemy to chemistry to physiology to the era of the gene. He saw the first use of ether for anesthesia. He saw medical fashion go from tight black coats buttoned to the neck to the denim jeans and scrub shirts worn today.

Standing in his REM state, Wags imagined absorbing the medical wisdom of centuries. He imagined the transfer of this knowledge with a single touch to the mummy's head, like a Mr. Spock mind-meld. *I would be brilliant*, he thought in his micronap.

A plot was born in a dream: The mummy would move to a new home. Considering the mummy's unnoticed state, we reasoned that the caper would go undetected from the inside for a while. Perhaps the wrinkled man who pushed the broom around the lecture hall, regularly knocking into the mummy's feet, would notice that his job was easier. We knew that the students and residents, who were always looking at note cards on clipboards, would fail to note the mummy's departure. So would the graying professors, whose heads bobbed with alternating sleep and attention during dull lectures.

Those who used the long bamboo stick pointer that resembled a Mark Twain character's fishing pole might notice the difference. Propped on the Padihershef's case, this pole had to go too. That was a bonus, because we were embarrassed when guest lecturers would be handed the wobbly, pockmarked stick to point at their famous data.

Post-call, Wags and I and sat on the brown couch; he was eating his usual Stouffer's TV dinner and I a greasy Banquet chicken with potato sticks when he told me of his microdream. A brilliant idea, the notion of the mummy capture consumed us for the next week. We joked that the mummy might even keep the mice at bay.

During our call time, we took detours to the wing of the hospital that held the mummy—a ghost town at night, empty and unlocked. We recorded the times the janitor made his late-night rounds, pinpointing the few hours after midnight as the time frame of opportunity. We rocked the mummy's case from side to side to get a sense of its weight. Bone dry, like a five-foot-tall Slim Jim, the mummy was surprisingly light, like stacked Egyptian cotton pillows—an easy move for a small hand truck and the two of us.

The mummy case was small; a few inches more than five feet high, two feet wide at the shoulders, and one foot wide at the feet. The case was ancient, with the dirty glass held in place by small glazing points that were loose and sharp. Although small, the mummy case was a foot too long to fit in either of our vehicles. We'd use a hand truck to take the mummy across the street and then up a stairwell to our apartment in Charles River Park, a street lane away. At night, a lone security guard watched the back door of our plotted egress.

Although there were big distinctions between the Gray Hairs and us, the line separating the foot soldiers—the residents, nurses, and security guards—was thin. The exposed and vulnerable face of the hospital to the public, we were interdependent. Security was essential, as the blue-shirted guards protected us from combative drunks, prisoners, and unruly patients and families. The security guards had a standard look—black hair slicked back, a brass badge, and starched medium-blue shirts with a patch of the hospital logo on one upper arm and the American flag on the other. Some wore black leather gloves without fingers. The guards helped us load our heavy metal-and-Plexiglas transport incubators in ambulances. They were also there to unload the precious cargo of infants when we returned.

Security was as much a part of EW action as we were. After 10:00 p.m. the drunks would come in. The guards would help subdue the combative patients brought in by police with lacerations or fractures that had occurred in falls or in wild, flailing fights.

Locked-leather restraints were as much a part of the emergency room equipment as the stretchers. Attached to stainless-steel bed frames, these restraints were our safety.

Once while working in the pediatric emergency room, I was punched in the eye by a wild six-year-old boy. The punch witnessed by an officer and the child pounced on by Security.

"No one hits our Docs!"

Security calls were common on the adult side and occasionally in pediatrics. One night I was on call with a junior resident. He was lanky and thoughtful, his words measured and his demeanor gentle. A mother brought in a five-year-old with fever. As the resident examined him, the child became combative. He screamed, he yelled, he punched his mother's chest.

I stepped out of the room. The resident said, "Allow the mother some time alone with him to let him calm down."

I told the mother, in her twenties, I would give her a few minutes alone to calm her son. Five minutes passed and I received the same violent response to my exam. This time, though, the mother began to yell at her boy "Stay still. They aren't doing anything to you." No matter what you try, child-physician phobia can't be easily overcome.

I made another attempt five minutes later, and again the child thrashed and the mother yelled. I stepped out again. This time, though, I heard screams coming from the exam room. Next we heard a slap, then the sound of a punch. We called Security—the young mother was attacking her son. That was the first and last time I saw a mother taken to Acute Psychiatric Services in leather restraints.

That evening we learned that she had a mental illness, Munchausen's syndrome by proxy, deriving pleasure from contriving illnesses for her son. This time, her son had refused to submit to another exam, to more unnecessary blood draws and pokes.

The guard who watched the back door at night owed us a favor; in fact, he owed us several. His father had a deteriorating neurologic condition that was taking his mind in a slow, sad way. Occasional falls and infections landed the guard's father in the emergency room. Admitted to the EW, the guard's father received VIP treatment. We'd give the guard, who couldn't afford even modestly priced items, the medications his father needed. We'd go into the medication closet empty-handed and come out with brown lunch bags stuffed with antibiotics and muscle relaxants.

One Wednesday night we told the guard we needed a favor. He appreciated our occasional pranks, some of which he learned about from dating the same nurses we did. We asked him to take a ten-minute break between 1:40 and 1:50 a.m. Hinting that the triage nurse, Nikki, was after him too, we told him to visit the main EW desk. Asking no questions, he trotted down the hallway.

Taking a hand truck from the basement storage room of the IF YOU LIVED HERE YOU'D BE HOME BY NOW apartment building, we scooted across the street through the hospital back door. Unwatched, we then crept into the lecture hall. After securing the mummy to the hand truck with surgical adhesive tape, we covered him with a starched white sheet. Within minutes we walked away with the mummy, glancing quickly right and left with nervousness.

Rolling the mummy's case across the street, we were invisible under the shadows of the dim orange sodium lamps. Into the side door, near a stairwell, we rolled the mummy as the loose glass panes rattled.

Back from his visit to the triage desk at 1:50 a.m., the guard sat at his desk near the back door. He didn't give a minute's thought to what we were up to. Perhaps he thought we were sneaking booze into the room across from the page operators. Perhaps he thought we were trying to impress young women with hospital tours during off-limits times. The notion that we'd steal a 2,500-year-old vestige of ancient Egypt was inconceivable.

Avoiding the elevator, we lifted the glass coffin up the back stairway. I was in the front, Wags in the back. We heard something fall inside the case, tap the glass, and then slide to the bottom. "Perhaps it was an ear," Wags joked. More likely, a glazing point had slipped.

Ten minutes later we had a new roommate standing proudly appreciated on Aunt Ida's rug, where he would watch our REM-inspiring naps. We talked about the generations and continents of wisdom he had absorbed over more than two thousand years.

With all we had learned in our collective schooling and would learn in our times to come on the Charles, Wags and I reflected that our combined knowledge would never be more than a pimple on the mummy's face.

The Bump

I'd never seen a two-year-old jumped before. This was no ordinary two-year-old, nor was East Boston an ordinary city. Johnny was born to a teenage mother. He came into this world screaming and wiggling, covered with the thick sticky paste of vernix pasted to his skin like all other children. But unlike other children, he had a large bump just above the bridge of his nose at birth.

The bump, about the size of a grape, protruded an inch from his forehead. It felt soft and moved when poked, like a pad of melting butter in a gold foil wrapper.

He was admitted to the pediatric ward, directly across from the room where the out-of-town SIDS babies roosted while waiting for their breathing studies. But the bump was a real problem, and we struggled to find its cause.

House officers, medical students, faculty, even the Gray Hairs, lined up to look at the infant, who was big at birth, ten pounds. They would walk in, press the bump, and walk out saying, "Interesting," which is hospital jargon for "I have no idea what's going on." Saying "interesting" conveys intelligence, signs of inner thought, brain gears moving, even though the brain gears were jammed in stupefaction.

In addition to the child's size and the bump, he had a look about him not seen in the other bulky babies who dotted our wards. His face was flat, and his eyes followed you around the room.

Big babies reached our units time and again, usually born to women with poorly controlled diabetes, whose sugar crossed the placenta to overfeed these babies in the womb. Large infants were typically placed in the neonatal intensive care units, hospitalized for drops in glucose levels.

How women gave birth to leviathan children was beyond our imagination; ten-, twelve-, and thirteen-pound babies plopped out. Collar bones would be broken or an arm dislocated. Yet with the hardiness of infancy come remarkable healing properties, and in a week these babies were fine.

Some of the nurses amused themselves and us with these babies, dressing the girls like performers in the circus, applying blue eye shadow. They fashioned dresses out of the crinkly exam-table paper sprinkled with glitter. They put bangles on the babies' wrists after the lights were down for the night.

Rounds kicked off in the early morning when the sun poked up, and the babies were arranged for their beauty pageant. Rounds over, the outfits came off and the infants were just babies again.

But Johnny wasn't touched by the night nurses. He was left alone and respected in his room, the center of curiosity. The nurses who fed him were the first to notice that although Johnny lay passive, there was no satisfying him when he ate.

A newborn takes two or three ounces of formula with each feeding, given every three hours. Three ounces for Johnny was a warm-up. Three ounces would go down in a blink, and then another three ounces would be swallowed just as fast, followed by loud, wet burps that rolled like thunder.

The snaps on his infant Onesie had to be undone as his stomach swelled. Even after drinking six or nine ounces, he clamored for more milk. We hypothesized that the bump was a tumor that extended into his hypothalamus, the brain's feeding center, causing excessive eating.

To see how far he could go in consumption, one senior resident instructed the baby's nurse to let him feed at will. After Johnny consumed fifteen ounces, the nurse declared, "No more."

Johnny loved to eat; each day he gained half a pound. As he sucked formula, his diapers overflowed onto the blue, plastic-covered short mattress below, the same type of mattress in our call rooms that made us sweat.

The parade of pokers and lookers was nearly gone when Dr. Peacock strolled in. With dramatic flair he said, "Tell me about this child." I explained the mysterious bump, the incessant appetite, and the wave of "interesting" summaries.

"You're wrong." He jousted. "You cannot separate hunger from thirst in an infant. How do you know the child is hungry, not thirsty?"

We then launched a "water deprivation test" to see if the child's appetite was caused by thirst from lack of the hormone vasopressin, the subject of his "pink-shirt" lecture. All fluids were withheld from Johnny, with a plan to measure his urine flow and the levels of blood salts every two hours.

Under the best of circumstances, water deprivation tests are a form of child abuse, as thirst is a primordial desire, protecting us from dehydration. Arranging for these tests was like preparing for a Papal visit. A nurse or nursing student is assigned to continuously watch the subject, guarding against surreptitious sips. Charts are posted with times the child is to be weighed and have blood taken, flagged with bright green and yellow Post-it Notes.

Then it began. The formula was withheld. A young nursing student wearing a red smock and a red-and-white nursing cap posted the first weight as we prepared for a ten-hour fast. Thirty minutes into the test, Johnny began to squirm in anticipation of the formula that wouldn't come. He murmured a bit, soft cries leaking out from mouth corners. Then the screams and wails followed, not the cries of newborns that make us feel sorry for them. No, these were intolerable screams that shook the floor and were relentless.

The nursing student standing guard came to tears. Seeing her trainee's discomfort, the battle-ax nursing instructor barked, "Pull yourself together! Only football players cry!" The young student imagined her nursing mentor flying off on her broom.

Dr. Peacock came by and upon hearing the screams said, "That's awful," imploring us to press on. And as nothing went in, urine came out, lots of it. Measuring the salts in urine and blood at the same time continued.

Dr. Peacock returned again, pointing at me. "If you figure out what is wrong with this infant, you can write him up and present him at society research meetings in two months." The prospect of making a presentation at a national meeting was intoxicating. The image of me standing on stage before the leaders in the field—brilliant men and women, geniuses, those who wrote the books I read—was tantalizing.

I too now stood guard at the door, flirting with the teary-eyed nursing student, ensuring that the covenant of the water deprivation test wasn't broken. After eight hours, we had our answer, dissecting the results of the chemistry panels as they came in.

Dr. Peacock appeared and announced, "Feed the baby!"

Like the Boston Fire Department flying to a blaze, the nursing team pounded down the corridor, formula-filled bottles in hand. Like fraternity "boat races," where frat members guzzle down cups of stale beer as quickly as possible, Johnny drained a succession of three-ounce bottles, which were left piled at his bedside.

I thought of the time my parents, unannounced, to their regret, visited one of my brothers at college in Philadelphia when he was his fraternity's boat race captain. "There he is!" said my proud father, waving as he strode forward in a wedding suit. Eighteen beers down, their son was steadying himself, hands on knees. Looking up, he said, "Mom. Dad. Hi," before vomiting at their feet. Lesson learned: Never make unannounced college visits.

The nursing student who cared for this child during the day kept saying "Another, another, another!" until the case of small bottles was empty. Then Johnny looked up and vomited, soaking the students' red smocks.

Not too long afterward, the neurosurgeons appeared. CT scans showed a tumor in the mysterious bump. This was the final part of the puzzle to be decoded.

Though a teenager, Johnny's mother was quick witted and smart; yet his medical complexity overwhelmed her. She fidgeted in anticipation, waiting for the test and diagnostic procedure results. She had to learn while mixing high school with raising her son.

After he left the hospital, Johnny's upbringing became increasingly difficult. As in the hospital, he drank and drank at home, gallons not quarts. At three months of age, he weighed twenty-five pounds. At one year of age, he weighed fifty pounds.

On his second birthday, he weighed more than his mother, a solid 110 pounds. She became depressed at the sight of her expanding son, and her own weight slipped by the week until Dr. Peacock took both mother and child under his supervision.

Far too big for infant clothing, Johnny was dressed in secondhand elementary school clothing. His belly protruded below midriff sweat-shirts with the Boston Celtics' leprechaun on the front. He was fit with specially designed high-top orthopedic baby shoes.

With his size, walking came late, and at a year and half he found his heels. A slow walker, he was pulled in a rusty wagon to the local park on top of a hill overlooking Boston. No stroller would hold him.

As he took unsteady, wide-leg steps, the other mothers and fright-ened children looked at him and whispered, "He's two!"

Occasionally, tough five- and six-year-olds ganged up on him. They knocked him down like one of those inflatable clowns with sand at the base. When his mother reported the kid muggings to the local police, the big-bellied commander responded by laughing. When we called in protest, he laughed at us too. "Doc, you do your job, I'll do mine."

Steadied by motherhood, though, she learned to become immune to the stares of neighbors. She had a child with a rare condition that fortu-nately had caught the attention of those who could provide answers.

The answer came via the scalpel of a gentleman neurosurgeon, who spoke with palms together like a minister. He explained the operation he was about to perform, how this could be a congenital tumor, how long the operation would take, and what her baby would be like after surgery.

After the operation, we met with the pathology team, learning that the mysterious lump was a collection of brain tissue. A tangle of neurons had grown out of a gap in the child's skull.

An abstract was prepared for a national meeting, where I envisioned I would present the mystery of Johnny, detailing an abnormal thirst center localized in brain tissue that had popped from his head. The meeting was to be in Las Vegas. I was given a ten-minute presentation slot. Dr. Peacock worked with me to polish my presentation, making me deliver it one hun-dred times until I was bored. I was granted two days off for the meeting; I was to deliver my address and fly back to Logan for call the next day.

I was nervous at the notion of presenting. Addressing a group of one thousand physicians further along in their careers than I, each posed to ask the perfect question, was terrifying. The evening before my talk, I again delivered it to Dr. Peacock. "Perfect," he said; "now, let's go out."

We wandered to the hotel lobby to see a show that was to begin at 11:00 p.m. Not having tickets, with his confident style, Dr. Peacock talked our way in. We now stood at the back of a packed room with round tables of ten seats each, wall to wall, packed from back to front. Only one table was open, far in the back.

"Let's sit here," pronounced Dr. Peacock, so we did. I couldn't see the opening act; we were too far back and I was nervously rehearsing my talk in my mind. Dr. Peacock whistled to a near-naked waitress to bring us drinks. "Not bad," he said. I didn't know if he was referring to the beer or the waitress.

Dr. Peacock spoke of another Las Vegas meeting. A spotlight with the intensity of a movie grand opening suddenly shined on the table.

"Laaaaadies and gentlemeeeen. We have a special guest with us tonight," the master of ceremony began. Dr. Peacock flattened his lapels, wondering how the MC knew he was there—a famous doctor from Man's Greatest Hospital!

"They must mean me," he said, taking a deep breath of pride. He backed his chair out and began to stand. Then he felt a strong hand on his right shoulder, pushing him back down in his seat.

"It's not for you, cowboy," said the man.

"Laaaaadies and gentlemeeeen. Let's have a special welcome for Mr. T!" the announcer said, making the *T* last ten seconds. Mr. T stood to take the spotlight alone. A strong black man with a Mandinka hairstyle and earrings, he was recognized to thunderous applause.

Dr. Peacock later capitalized on the moment when colleagues at the show said, "I didn't know you and Mr. T were such good friends."

"Of course we are," he said with a chest puff.

Mr. T wanted to know why he was at this table. Dr. Peacock explained who he was and that he was from Man's Greatest Hospital. Dr. Peacock then told me to tell Mr. T about the baby with the mysterious bump. Mr. T began listening to the story with fascination. "That's weirder than Hollywood," he said, before we were escorted from the table.

Show over, at 1:00 a.m. we hit the casinos. I loaned Dr. Peacock twenty dollars for slot machines, which he lost. Six hours later, I gave my talk, my nervousness gone.

After my ten-minute talk was over, the audience asked only three simple, self-inflating questions. My presentation went well, but my talk was ranked second in the house-officer category. I stood on the podium behind a resident from Brown who had helped discover anticlotting agents from hookworms. I was runner-up again.

I hopped a jet home, reflecting during a nap-filled flight on my academic debut. During the flight, I wondered what I could have done better to take the top prize.

I saw the mouth of the Charles and Boston Harbor as my jet landed. And then I was back on call that night.

Several years later, in late-night reruns, I was watching an episode of *The A-Team*. There was Mr. T battling a criminal with an unusual look. *What is that,* I asked myself? It was a bump between the villain's eyes! Mr. T head-butted the criminal and planted his thumb into the bump, wiggling his thumb side to side. The villain dropped to the ground, unconscious. Was Dr. Peacock still in cahoots with Mr. T.?

The Prince of Darkness

At the evening meal, I met Wags with the rest of the night-call crew, recanting the stories of my first presentation. Sputum Man and the Gypsies tried to listen, but they were kept at bay as Sputum Man filled five cups than night, not his usual three.

The previous evening, Wags had run into his own celebrity. "The Artist formerly known as Prince" came to Boston, which happened rarely, and gave a surprise show at a club behind Fenway Park on Lansdowne Street.

Classic rock clubs were huge, with beer-soaked dance floors. Here Boston's young met and danced while videos of Duran Duran and Michael Jackson were projected on big white walls. These clubs held hundreds of patrons. Being on the other side of town from our home base, we visited these clubs less than our favorites at Faneuil Hall.

These clubs had dress codes for men but none for women. Going to Metro one night with one of the Cathys, I showed up at the door in sneakers; she sported red high heels.

"She can go in. You can't. No sneakers for guys," said the bouncer in a tight black T-shirt. To the end of the line we went, switching shoes along the way. Our turn came again, Cathy in sneakers and me in red pumps. With my heels hanging over the shoe counters, we shuffled in.

While I was away in Vegas, Wags was in the EW covering for the perpetrator of the Rose Kennedy hoax, who had been suspended. We thought he was safe from more than verbal reprimand until he was discovered off-hours in OR3 with the wife of a hospital administrator. His weeklong suspension only did him good; others were assigned to shoulder his call and work.

We were worshippers of Prince, his lyrics touching our core. His sexual lyrics were temporal messages for us. *Little Red Corvette* was our party anthem. That night, Prince was playing at Metro. Wags had tickets, painfully surrendering them when assigned call that night.

At 1:00 a.m., a thin man with black curly hair and wearing tight purple leather came to the hospital door. He didn't say much and checked in as Mike Barnicle. Wags imagined it was Prince, thinking how, during the show, he was duck-walking across the stage in little staccato steps when his metal microphone base swung up, gashing his right brow. But the patient didn't tell Wags how he cut his eyelid and Wags didn't pursue it. Wags only knew it was his turn for sewing.

Like Mr. T with me, the thin man in purple was interested in Wags, what we did in the OR, how we coped with the horrible things we saw. Taking care of the rich and famous in a hospital for the rich and famous, we learned they were no more medically sophisticated than the others sitting in the emergency room. The rich and famous, though, enjoyed talking to us about disciplines so different from theirs.

Cleaning the wound and sewing the laceration, Wags talked about where he went to medical school, the long hours he worked, the daily grind that wore him down, the man who died as he interviewed him.

Then Wags slipped. Blabbing on as we do, the purposeful distraction that makes patient anxiety fade, he mentioned that we had a mummy in our apartment. The man being sewn stopped humming and stared at him.

From that time on, Wags could have completed the simple suturing without local anesthetic. The man in purple was spellbound. He was interested in the afterworld, and his fascination with the mummy exploded.

"How old was the mummy?" he asked. "Male or female?. What did it die from?"

And then he asked, "Can it help me connect with the afterlife?"

Wags answered the last questions with a soft Southern laugh, saying "Suuure." He put a bandage over the small wound sewn with four sutures and gave the man in purple wound-care instructions.

He asked Wags for his phone number, promising he'd be in touch.

As the man in purple was reading his wound-care instruction sheet, Wags said one last thing. "If ya return, I'll introduce you to our girl named Nikki."

"*Really!*" said the patient with a wink.

When I measured Wags's story about meeting possible Prince against mine with Mr. T, I knew I was trumped.

I was runner-up again.

Duck Fires

I was told by the senior surgical resident, who was rotating at the burn center, that they used to light ducks on fire and that's how the accident happened. Of course the story was true; it came from a senior resident.

The brothers lived on a farm in Utah, an hour from Park City. Eight and ten years old, each boy blamed the other. Early in the evening on summer days, they would creep up to nests of sleeping ducks, squirt lighter fluid on them, and toss a match. They would then jump, yelling "Cool!" as the flaming birds flew off.

Usually the ducks were lucky. The fluid burned off in seconds and they winged away, left with a few scattered clumps of scorched feathers. Other ducks, soaked preflight, fell from the sky like shooting stars. The boys' attacks were so pervasive that local duck hunters reported problems in the duck population to the local fish-and-game regulatory agencies, reporting the new ducks with curly feathers.

The boys became bolder and coordinated surprise attacks on groups of sleeping birds, watching clusters of flaming birds hit the skies. As before, some ducks flamed out and winged off; others corkscrew spun to the ground.

Our child development lectures taught us, "Watch for the child who abuses animals. This type of pathological behavior is the harbinger for an adult life of crime and incarceration." We were told how Charles Manson used to shave cats and how Albert DeSalvo, the Boston Strangler, used to garrote baby goats. We were told how Richard Speck, who killed nursing students in Chicago, put stockings on dogs and that Jeffrey Dahmer had sex with animals before eating their livers.

After six months of torturing ducks and hunters charting the new duck disease, "curly feather blight," the boys set their sight on larger prey. They decided to attack Canada geese, the heavy birds of majestic V-formation flight. "Charcoal lighter fluid won't be enough," said the older boy. So they moved up the petrochemical combustion ladder to gasoline.

Gasoline is more combustible and has a lower flashpoint than the kerosene in lighter fluid, but the boys didn't know this. Their squirt cans of lighter fluid empty, they snuck into their grandfather's barn and siphoned fuel from a blue Ford tractor.

Early in the evening, they snuck up on a roost of sleeping geese, unloaded their squirt cans, and tossed a match at the hissing and charging ganders.

Whoosh! A huge flash followed, with the flames traveling up the stream of fluid until it hit the squirt nozzle. The geese erupted in flight, flapping gas-soaked wings and beating off drops of burning gas. Next, the two squirt cans exploded, showering the boys in flaming gasoline. The boys' grandfather heard the back-to-back booms and looked outside to see two flames running across a field and other sets of flames moving twenty feet off the ground.

"What the hell's goin' on?" he yelled.

He heard the boys screaming as they ran toward him. Following instinct, he ran toward them, hobbling from a war injury. He reached the boys, knocked them to the ground, and rolled them in the field to extinguish the flames. He glanced up and saw a screaming goose flying low until it crashed into a bush that then ignited. The other family members ran from the white farmhouse too, seeing the burning bush and smelling the horrible odor of burnt skin, hair, feathers, and hay.

The next day the boys were at our burn center, with burns over 95 percent of their bodies. Only their armpits had been spared.

Our rotations at the burn center left an indelible impact on the pediatricians and surgeons who cared for burned children. The children were secluded in isolation rooms with blue plastic tents. These rooms were close to the ORs, where the dead and burned skin was shaved off daily until live tissue that bled was found.

The Utah boys were in beds next to each other. IV lines and saline solutions were running into their arms. The shocked parents told the story of the fowl fires to the parents of the other children at the center, who next told their own foul tales.

Wags was the intern rotating in the burn center the month the boys arrived and was part of the team that took them to the operating room to remove the burned skin and plan their recovery. I too spent time at that center, where seemingly no-hope kids would walk out the door months later with proud smiles, albeit some crooked from scars. Along with the dead tissue, the surgeons shaved the remaining fresh pink armpit skin, layering it in round glass culture dishes that went to a special laboratory. The skin would be cultured and expanded, to be used to re-cover the children.

The next night Wags was eating a TV dinner pulled from an orange box and I was eating my greasy chicken. He told me about the duck-fire boys and how they were going to grow skin from their unburned armpits to re-cover them. As he told the story, the mummy peered at him.

"Let's ask Padihershef what he would do!" Wags joked.

While Wags was in the burn center, I was on a rotation of different pediatric subspecialists—a Whitman's Sampler of dermatology, nephrology, and endocrinology. The first week, I was in dermatology, learning how to treat pimply-faced kids, eczema, and warts.

Making warts vanish was gratifying. Using a scalpel blade, I slowly shaved skin layers until I saw the dark in the middle of the verruca, the feeding blood vessel that kept the wart alive. I then slapped occlusive tape over the wart. Two weeks later the wart was gone, its absence greeted by smiling faces.

Wags told me about his procedure of the day; I told him of my mistake of the day. I was in Dr. Peacock's endocrine clinic seeing a ten-year-old boy who was deficient in growth hormone. He was receiving injections of replacement hormones to bring him to the height of his classmates. During my encounter with the boy, I noticed that his knuckles were covered with warts of different sizes, the pimpled look of a toad's back.

"How do you feel about your warts?" I asked.

"I hate them," answered the boy.

One week a dermatologist, I said, "I can help you."

I took a fresh scalpel from the top drawer, along with gauze, white tape, and gloves. Over the next fifteen minutes, eleven warts were shaved, blotted with stiff gauze, and covered. The procedure done, he was sent three floors down to Radiology for an X-ray of his hand, which would predict his remaining growth.

Dr. Peacock received a call from Radiology.

"Your patient is hemorrhaging," the technician said.

Looking baffled, Dr. Peacock said, "Send him up."

The boy was back in the same exam room where I had shaved the warts. His hands were wrapped in white towels provided by the X-ray technicians; the towels were checkerboard red, like a Midwest water tower.

"I forgot to tell you, I have hemophilia," the boy said.

I immediately sent the boy down to the EW. An IV was placed and clotting agents were infused to stop the bleeding. Dr. Peacock had a clinic bursting with complicated patients and forgot about the bleeding boy. I didn't bring it up either.

Wags shaved things too. Gowned in blue OR garb, he debrided skin using a bright silver device that looked like a cheese grater. The duck-fire boys were in the operating room every day having their wounds cleaned, the burned skin shaved to where pink and red tissue was found. Back from the ORs, they were soon in their sterile rooms, nurses in blue scrubs transferring bags of IV fluids to stainless steel stanchions at the bedside.

These events occurred every day in a ward of children, each with a story behind his or her catastrophe. There was a boy from Maine who was dipping slaughtered chickens in a pot of boiling water at the family farm to remove feathers. A leg on the black metal tripod stand snapped and a hundred gallons of boiling water spilled onto his belly and legs, causing his skin to peel in minutes.

A thirteen-year-old boy from Queens had been playing in a subway yard. He stepped on the third rail of a subway line, an electrified conduit carrying high-voltage electricity. As his right foot stepped on the charged rail, his left foot touched a steel rail eighteen inches over. A circuit completed, all the tissues from the right to the left foot were seared in an instant.

Although the work was depressing, technically the month went well for Wags. The kids in his care looked like mummies, except the wrappings on the burn center children were bright white, not faded tan cotton like our mummy's.

A week to go in his burn center rotation, Wags came home overjoyed. The laboratory had succeeded in growing several yards of new skin from the boys' armpit skin, which had escaped immolation. In five days the new skin was to be layered on the exposed muscles and fascia that pleaded for a covering.

As we talked over TV dinners, an idea flashed. What would happen when the boys reached puberty? Would the skin cells that would soon cover the boys sprout hair and stink like armpits?

The next day Wags talked to his senior resident about our concern. Some surgeons, Wags found, were dismissive of any notion that wasn't theirs, no matter how brilliant or practical. His senior was one of those closed-minded surgeons.

I ran our worries by Dr. Peacock. He said there was one way to find out what was going to happen and placed a vial of testosterone propionate in my hand. The next night, Wags was on call and I was off for the evening. I met him in the burn center lobby, and we went up the backstairs to the laboratory where the cells grew. At night the laboratory was empty. The staff technicians and scientists worked 9:00 a.m. to 5:00 p.m., the rational hours of the non-trainee medical world.

We peered into the warm and humid incubators packed with large flasks containing the armpit cells. We pulled out a few plates and, in a sterile tissue culture hood, added testosterone to some dishes, which we marked with a Sharpie and replaced in the incubator.

We planned to inspect the experimental specimens two days later. But the day before the new skin was to be applied in layers, the lab team arrived for surprising nighttime work. They began layering the cultivated skin on a special collagen matrix that would be applied to the boys.

We planned to look for budding hairs and smell whether the dishes produced the foul whiff of a teenage armpit. We were too late and couldn't yank the plates to make sure that the testosterone-treated cells became part of the cell pool to cover the brothers the next morning. Maybe they were, maybe they weren't—we did not know.

Dr. Peacock called at night and asked what we had learned. I explained that we couldn't follow up, but left out the explanation.

The first of the duck boys was in the OR at 6:00 a.m. The target sites of the new skin, the abdomen and legs, were prepared. The ooze of open wounds was removed and the dermis below scraped to make it bleed to feed the new cells. The growing cells on their matrix scaffold came out next. As the incubator door opened, the lead technician wrinkled his nose saying, "Yikes. This smells like my son's hockey skates."

"Interesting. I'm sure it's nothing," remarked the senior surgeon. Just cell-matrix interaction."

The new skin lay on the bottom of the dishes covered by pink, clear media. A technician smoothed the floating tissue with blunt-tipped forceps. The plates were loaded on a stainless-steel cart and wheeled to the OR.

Layered in patches, the skin went down, moist and glistening. Like a quilt, pieces were cut into precise squares and opposed each other. Wags patiently applied the patches of new skin. Being the junior team member, he was applying skin to the lower leg. His sudden wide-eyed look caught the attention of the senior surgeon, who asked, "Wags, is everything okay?"

"Sure," Wags answered. "I'm just trying to be sure everything is okay, sir." He didn't mention what he saw on the skin patch that he had just applied. The sodding done, the grafts were covered with moist white gauze.

The next Friday we were both on call and met in the basement cafeteria. This meal we sat by ourselves, no plans to be made, as this was the start of forty-eight hours on. Whispering, Wags described several crops of budding hairs on the bellies and legs of the boys. The blessing of the new skin came with a curse that would remain latent until the boys' teenage years.

Our times at the burn center taught Wags and me that bad judgment and bad luck both took their toll on children. And when I reflected on our time there, I sifted through my thoughts to find ways to stop both.

But when we told our young patients, "You need to protect yourself from yourself," they would only look up and say, "Huh?"

Bath Time

Our trips to Fenway had ended after the leaves turned autumn orange and red and dropped to streets, clogging sewers. As the sunlight of the day shortened, Wags and I became more comfortable with the responsibility of ministering medicine to the infirm. Only months from medical school graduation, though, we sank into months of unenthusiastic work as the nights lengthened and our sleep debt grew like compound interest.

Wags continued to experiment with different TV dinners. The local supermarket charged twice the prices of the suburban stores in Arlington or Newton. It was there Wags met a woman who worked in the finance district. He said they glanced at each other in the frozen food section, the next aisle over from the nut section Wags frequented. Instantly attracted, the two strangers were pulled together in an invisible bond of horniness.

Wags and Melissa became inseparable for the next two months, consuming his free time during off-call day. She was quiet, afraid to speak to me, perhaps feeling guilty that she was supplanting my good friend's companionship. She also hated the mummy and sat or stood far from the glass case.

She would wait until I wasn't in the apartment, then hurry over to have sex with Wags in her favorite spot, his bathtub. I'd return post-call to find puddles in the hallway. Soggy cardboard toilet paper cores were out there too, washed out of the bathroom by waves generated by belly slaps.

I couldn't imagine a more unhygienic locale for sex than Wags's bathroom—the home of turquoise stalactites that hung from Head & Shoulders bottles and carpeted with cardboard toilet paper cores. A black ring like volcanic ash outlined his tub, the remnants of oxidized soap.

Nevertheless, Wags boasted that when Melissa visited, she'd fill the tub, hop in, and they would go at it. She had no fear of Wags's fraternity hygiene. After sex, they dressed, watched TV over TV dinners, and then she left. She had no interest in movie dates or Beacon Hill dinners.

Once one of the Cathys met Melissa; since Melissa had trouble with small talk, the conversation was short, something about shoes. When I told Cathy of Melissa's modus operandi, she shuddered. No Cathy chanced entering Wags's bathroom, not even to empty an overfull bladder.

While Wags was drowning with Melissa, I was on my own. I would occasion the homes of the married. Whereas the single residents ventured out on the town on free nights, the married residents stayed in for well-prepared meals that outmatched the cheap restaurants a short walk away that I frequented. Over dinner, the wives of the residents, most of whom weren't in medicine, asked about my tough cases and how tired I was—innocent questions seeking affirmation and confirmation of their husbands' sleep deprivation and depression.

After dinner, sometimes we'd play Trivial Pursuit or Stratego, games that allowed us to show our strength of intellect. These nights usually ended around 10:00 p.m., not the late-night no-curfew hours of the single.

As Wags and I drifted through different girls, I was envious of the solid relationships of the married house officers. The married house officers, betrothed just before the start of residency or halfway through medical school, stood together with their spouses through the tough times, adding stability and strength to each other.

The co-intern from Johns Hopkins, who was paired with me for most of my rotations, married halfway through medical school. His wife was from Malaysia and was married wearing a traditional red gown. When she told her father that she was marrying a non-Asian, her father said, "Harumph," not caring that the groom was a star medical student.

There were married residents in medicine, pediatrics, and surgery, their partners sharing the sacrifice of different kinds of training. These house officers had a degree of civility and properness that this single didn't have. There was no sex in gross bath tubs or OR3.

When I told my married friends about how Wags and I spent our spare time, the wives laughed politely, counting their lucky stars that they had probity in their husbands. But they were more aghast than amused.

When I was on my own, one of my favorite restaurants was an Italian eatery on Cambridge Avenue, owned by two young men who worked days and nights that rivaled ours. One day the cooking grease that had splattered on the back wall above the industrial steel stove caught fire. Because the restaurant was located next door to the firehouse, the flames should have been put out fast, with just a bit of greasy smoke damage. But the fire company was out on a false alarm, and when the trucks returned, the restaurant was in full blaze. Three months passed before the young owners could restart their livelihood.

Across the street from the hospital was a bar on the corner, where patients would escape for a shot of whiskey or a smoke. The bar manager would call hospital security when patients arrived with IV poles and crystalline solutions dripping into their veins.

Between the Italian restaurant and the hospital bar was a gay club without windows or a sign, just a plain brown door. You'd walk by that door a hundred times not knowing there was a dazzling bar inside. But as the night moved on, men and women would stand smoking on the sidewalk, jumping back inside when the last drag on a cigarette was done.

During the day the club was open, but no one stood outside. The lone exception was when the Gay Pride Parade came up Cambridge Street in June. The gum-spotted sidewalk in front of the club would be lined with men and women whistling at the floats of beefy men dressed in leather and feathers as Wagner's *Tannhäuser* repeated over loudspeakers.

I saw my sailing instructors at the club. A former rower, past racing prime, I still craved the water. Desiring to learn to sail, I joined the community sailing program twenty yards from the Hatch Shell along the Charles River. I was greeted at the reception desk by a stern woman who asked, "Have you sailed before?"

"No. That's why I'm here," I answered.

"How old are you?" she asked, following with, "Have you ever sailed before? Can you swim?"

Can you, can you, can you? I thought, *Why the interrogation?*

On the water, the humiliation continued. I was paired with an instructor who would try to transform me from rower to sailor—looking ahead, not backward. I learned that my instructors didn't like the Boston medical personnel, and they let sail booms slip to whack the back of my head. After two weeks, my dreams of sailing the Charles were gone.

Some of the single residents tired of the girl-chasing lifestyle, not realizing they too were being pursued by women seeking matrimony and a doctor's dowry. Wags's Melissa wasn't that way. She was a simple, introverted girl who had just discovered her sexuality as she was learning to toss her inhibitions away.

Among the doctor-chasers was a surgical floor nurse with dyed blond hair and big white teeth that she framed with bright red lipstick. She slept with resident after resident, looking for a vulnerable one.

The vulnerable one was the quiet blond-haired intern from Indiana, who kept to himself, not dating much. Six weeks after she snared him, they were engaged to be married the next month.

She developed appendicitis on the night of their wedding, and he drove her to the hospital in her wedding gown. Two months later they were divorced. But after the nullification, the resident no longer kept to himself, joining us for trips to the downtown bars, liberated from conservative values that marriage was the only way to relationships.

After a while, Melissa and Wags calmed down. The puddles on the floor were fewer and smaller. Cardboard rolls no longer washed out into the hallway. The now-confident Melissa was off for other adventures with other men.

Wags and I were now back in each other's good company, and on no-call night we bounded out to the Boston bars again. As he told me of Melissa's departure, I imagined her moving on to someone else—perhaps someone with a Jacuzzi.

Under Your Breath

Working the wards and the EW, we were the hospital's front line, and we learned the nuances of being hospital public relations officers. Sometimes the public persona of the house officer needed a bit of smoothing. One lesson in public relations started when a pediatric resident muttered, "And you can go fuck yourself" to the mother of a child with a hyphenated last name.

The boy—blond hair, blue eyes, and cherry-red cheeks—was referred to the pediatric EW for "just a throat culture."

"This is all I want. My pediatrician sent me. I don't want my child examined," the mother demanded.

But that wasn't how we worked. We were a full-service, if not an extra-full-service, evaluation center, not a diagnostic center for the pediatrician's whim.

"I'm sorry, that's not what we do here. Your child needs to be evaluated," said the resident.

"That's not what my doctor said!" the mother answered.

Parent disputes were common. We against parents, who grudgingly arrived on our doorstep after calling their pediatricians and being told, "You should go to the hospital. I'll telephone. They will take you right in."

They knew that last part was a lie.

Parents dismayed at the prospect of having to take their children to the EW, thoughts they never relayed to their doctor, would say, "Of course doctor, we'll go immediately." There was no hint of the dissent swimming in their minds. Most parents knew how the game was played and were grudgingly appreciative of us. But others would come in armed with mental shotguns.

But as parents soon learned, we could never take them right in. It was not because we didn't want to, but we had a limited number of exam rooms. Febrile and drooping kids would need to sit in a stuffed waiting area until a room opened.

They were here to see us once. No gray hair like their local physician, for some we were fair game for attacks. These parents saw us as adversaries not healers, the ones who would heap procedures and wasted time on them and their child.

I supposed the parent protectiveness was justified. You'd never know if the intern or resident who saw you was a star or a slug, fresh or sleep deprived, up for a day or two or not, or had steady hands or a shake. My father used to joke, "What do they call someone who graduates last in his medical school class? *Doctor!*"

They also had to contend with several layers of care. First was the triage nurse, some who worked at 78 RPM and others at 16 RPM. In our area we had the 16 RPM version, Eda, a chubby, plodding woman from Britain. She didn't obfuscate with deliberation, she obfuscated with slowness. She walked slowly, talked slowly, took vital signs slowly—all while wearing a white uniform that commanded respect.

Tasks that took others ten minutes took her thirty. As the waiting room was packed with children sweaty and wheezing, some with stool dripping down their pant legs, she controlled room flow. Part of her responsibility was to circle the waiting room, looking for children sitting on their parents' laps about to decompensate. Her time with us ended when she failed to recognize a severely septic child, 105-degree fever and listless. The boy went into shock before the gasps of the other waiting parents. The child nearly died, fortunately later recovering in our intensive care unit.

This night Eda was on, and the resident was frustrated with the things he couldn't control—the nurse and a request for a service we didn't provide. He told the mother again that the child had to be examined, to which she responded, "I'm going to call my doctor now."

Muttering, not meaning to be heard, he then said, "And you can go fuck yourself too." It was one of those thoughts we think we're thinking and not saying, but he said it.

"I'm really going to call my doctor now!" said the mother, and call and call she did. She rang her pediatrician, the department chair, and the hospital president.

What would the repercussions be? A tongue-lashing, a letter of apology? He said what he wanted to, when we usually rolled our tongues in.

In a different act of defiance, the Checkmark Surgeon used to walk around with a pocket full of quarters. If staff and nurses mouthed off to him, he pulled out a shiny quarter, placed it in their palm, and said, "Here, go buy yourself a personality."

But what came of his actions? Just the loss of a few coins, because he had made his point.

I too allowed my emotions to get the better of me in the EW. A disabled boy I had cared for when his fever hit 108 degrees the week earlier was transferred from another hospital with a mid-forearm fracture. On his arrival, there was no splint, and his forearm was at a right angle.

I picked up the phone and called the transferring nurse.

"The child came in with his fractured arm at a right angle! No splint! This is malpractice!"

The next day my Chair paged me. A page from the top wasn't good, never to be answered with alacrity. Paged again, I answered.

Then came the "Did you or did you nots."

"Did you or did you not call the Sommerville Emergency Room last night?

"Did you or did you not speak to the triage nurse?

"Did you or did you not say the child arrived without a splint?

"Did you or did you not say that was malpractice?

"Did you or did you not consider all possibilities?

"Did you or did you not consider that the mother removed the splint?

"Well, you're being sued for libel and slander. The transferring physician is collecting affidavits saying that the infant was splinted prior to transfer."

The woodshed act over, my Chair made phone calls. I wrote a note of apology; lesson learned.

Lessons were learned by parents too. Many EW visits were related to viruses, accidents, or dog bites, and sometimes the parents were to blame. One night a baby came in, six weeks old, feeding poorly and flaccid. The heart monitor clocked the heartbeat at 150 beats per minute. The baby was seen by a "causal" junior resident who wasn't concerned. The Compulsive Resident came in next and listened to the infant's heart.

"The heart rate is 300, not 150!" he said. "The EKG is picking up every other beat. *Who turned down the monitor gain?*"

The cardiologist arrived, black haired with a trim black beard, and serious. He reached into the father's shirt pocket and pulled out a pack of cigarettes. He crumpled them in one squeeze, threw them on the floor, and stomped on them, twisting his foot over the pack for thirty seconds.

"You did this! Your smoking triggered the arrhythmia in your child. You're going to kill your baby," he said before turning his back to walk out.

We blocked the tachycardia with an ice bag placed in the baby's face, a maneuver that triggers over-activation of the vagus nerve to the heart, slowing the heart rate and breaking the arrhythmia—simplicity in medicine.

The dog bite lessons were also tough to make parents grasp. When a dog mauled a child's arm or face, parents usually blamed the child.

"He stepped on Aussie's tail."

"He took Shaggy's toy."

"He patted Scruffy when she was eating."

They never seemed to get it and kept their child-biting pets at the expense of their children.

"We've had Buzzy longer than Tommy," they'd say. "Doctor. How can we get rid of him?"

Sewing up one boy with face bites from a Chow, I asked, "What is your dog's name?"

"Cujo," he answered.

They kept the dog.

Right or wrong, it seemed to us that adopted dogs were the most dangerous. We see these dogs in cameo spots in newspapers ads that say, "Take me home or they'll gas me." Terriers with droopy ears and smiling Dalmatians wearing fire hats, displayed for the public to weep over and take home. These dogs found their way to the pounds for reasons the canines could never tell.

After I saw a boy's face mangled by an adopted Airedale, scars he would wear the rest of his life, I asked parents of the children I cared for, "Do you have a dog? Was it adopted?"

If the answer was yes, I would say, "Get rid of it!"

But most parents laughed, not believing I was serious. My department Chair fielded calls from the parents who did believe I was serious. I didn't care; I'd seen my share of mauling.

You never could guess who or what disease would come through the EW door. Some patients came directly from Logan airport after transatlantic flights to have their failing child's problem diagnosed.

One girl showed up from outside Ferrara, Italy. At thirteen years old, she was a head shorter than her sister, three years her junior. She came with stacks of X-rays, including a scan of her brain showing a tumor in the front part. "Doctor, can you help her?" the parents asked,

She was admitted and found to have a craniopharyngioma compressing her pituitary gland, which controls growth and puberty. She stayed with us for a month. The tumor was removed and replacement medicines were given. A child reborn, she went back to Italy. She died a year later from adrenal insufficiency, a complication of pituitary disease. We warned the local doctors about this risk, but our pleas didn't register.

One evening I was working with a young superstar to be. He had an MD and a PhD from Cornell. The inventor of the "muffled beeper sign." He was overweight, and his sides hung over his belt and beeper. He had to lean to starboard to hear a page. Dr. Peacock called saying, "I'm sending you a baby without a thyroid. Get him started on thyroxin right away!"

Aye, aye, sir! I thought.

However, the child wasn't as billed. His temperature was 104 degrees on arrival, so he was at risk for a bacterial infection. Thus, more than thyroid medication, he needed blood, urine, and spinal fluids sampled and cultured.

No words send fear into a parent like "spinal tap."

"We need to do a spinal tap."

"We need to do a spinal tap to see if there's meningitis."

"We need to do a spinal tap or your baby will die."

The "spinal tap–meningitis" combo was more than most parents could bear.

"Please, do you have to?"

"Will he be brain damaged afterward?"

"How many times have you done this before?"

"Will you wear a mask and gloves?"

"Yes, your baby needs a spinal tap, and yes, your baby will be fine afterward."

This time the spinal tap took a while. As part of the process, infants are bent like commas, with someone looking at their face to be sure the flexed heads don't block their floppy airways. You look at the hips, feel for the spot between the vertebrae, and bingo, a two-inch needle slides in and the most beautiful fluid you'll ever see drains, clear like a mountain stream.

Not this time. The young scholar couldn't hit the intervertebral space.

"Another needle please."

No luck.

"Let's reposition the baby."

Right side, left side, sitting up, he had no luck. At last a drop of blood fluid dripped; "a bad tap," the drop was placed in a culture tube to be sent to laboratory.

Swaddled, the infant was given back to the mother.

"No problem."

The next week I was at the endocrine conference with Dr. Peacock. In mean-grandmother fashion, he wagged his finger at me while fifteen other physicians in the room sat giddy.

"Twelve fractures! That's what they gave my baby," said Dr. Peacock.

The baby wasn't moving the day after the lumbar puncture, and a bone scan was ordered. Unknown to us and to Dr. Peacock, the baby also had osteogenesis imperfecta, or "OI," where bone strength is weak and fractures can occur with incidental contact. The baby was started on thyroid hormone; the fractures healed, and the infant went home and did well.

The pain of what we did lingered in us. How were we to know the hidden unknowns of medicine? How were we to know the unknown harm that would be our fault, now and throughout our careers?

In the midst of lining, tubing, poking, and culturing, there was always EW relief. One attending fit himself into the round silver garbage can where we tossed bloody gauze, half-eaten bananas, and crumpled notes. He would rock back and forth saying "I'm R2-D2," the *Star Wars* character.

On Sunday mornings, we'd take the insets from the *Boston Globe*—the part packed with circulars from which shut-ins order embroidered washcloths, personalized name stamps, and other junk that never finds its way to store shelves.

We enrolled our peers in the Porcelain Unicorn of the Month Club, the Music Box of the Month Club, and the Jellies from Argentina of the Month Club. We ordered Capodimonte figurines like those seen on the blue-screen specials of late-night television. The Last Supper set, the most expensive, was the least well received.

We adulterated the photos of house officers that hung on the walls. We applied Hitler-style moustaches on some and blackened teeth on others. We added pearls and bandanas too.

We hacked into the laboratory reporting system and created test results for our coresidents stating "Gonorrhea culture: positive. High bacterial count." We put the printed results in an unsealed envelope and pinned it to the wall. Under the house officer's name we placed a big red CONFIDENTIAL stamp, knowing the more stamps, the more it would be read by the curious. Then the rumors started.

"Do you think she caught it from him?"

"I heard he also slept with Julie. Should we tell her? She's our friend."

"And her too?"

With the exuberance and excitement of twenty-four hours on and twenty-four hours off day after day came episodes of horrible sadness. Death always rode through the EW.

There was a small room near the entrance where families would wait while husbands, wives, aunts, uncles, grandparents, and children were "coded," the act of trying to bring life back to the suddenly dead.

There are many more codes on the adult than the pediatric side. When "pedi codes" came in, they went to the surgical or trauma bays, where we worked together.

The modest room up front had seating for two, and most relatives stood in grief. A social worker would hold their hands, passing the stiff hospital tissues around in a circle. We dubbed that room the "Tear Drop

Lounge." Here families learned that the cycle of life was complete, never a spot one wanted to be.

The end of life was uncanny at times. We were a half mile from the sagging Boston Garden, or "Gaahden"—a building as hallowed as it was decaying, a musty building of parquet floors where Larry Bird knew how to get the upper hand with quirky floor bounces. It had big yellow air ducts zigzagging above, which we banged on during rallies. There were exposed steel rafters. The building was a site of fuses, flaking electric boxes, and fraying wiring with cloth insulation.

There was a big penalty to be paid if you stuck a screwdriver in the wrong spot. Electrocuted Boston Garden workers were transported with exit wounds of lightning out the back of their skulls, leaving their cerebellum open.

One Halloween we saw a fellow dressed like Frankenstein's monster with white and green face paint and a noose around his neck. He went to a party at a local pub. Drunk on a bar table, he jokingly swung his rope over a rafter. Then the legs of the table kicked out. He was brought in coding, cardiac compressions given, his face now white, green, and blue.

The saddest losses were the accidental deaths of children. One girl was brought in by ambulance unconscious, blood dripping from her ears after a book shelf toppled on her in daycare. At her side bent a pediatrician, his gray hair in a ponytail, the first responder from the physician's office next door. She had a basilar skull fracture and brain stem hemorrhage; we couldn't do much.

The pediatrician waited quietly by the child's side until the parents arrived. He wiped his face and then joined the parents in the Tear Drop Lounge.

After the codes and the deaths, there was pure respect for the family and the decedents. We ensured that last moments rang precious before the long trip to the basement morgue with stainless steel lockers. If physicians or nurses told you they shed no tears, they were lying.

But after these sad events visited our days of training, we'd brush ourselves off and bounce back to be the smiling face of the hospital. Tired and loose tongued, we were back at it again—the young and the distressed-less.

Problem Child

One would assume that after the testing, interviews, and review committees to select those who would train at Man's Greatest Hospital—those vetted from the hundreds who'd apply—each trainee would be a star, the future of our field. Wags and I wondered how we survived the white-knuckle interview process to train where so many others dreamed of training, only to be told no.

The culling processes varied with department. The surgical candidates sat at a table ringed with Gray Hairs. Questions were asked, to be answered while the young aspiring surgeons tied knots with silky suture material.

"What are the signs of acute bowel obstruction?"

"What's the weight of a gallbladder?"

"What does the pudendal nerve innervate?"

"Should alcoholics be transplanted?"

Medical residency applicants took tests in addition to their interviews. Clad in black suits on interview day, they resembled funeral home staff more than physicians and one-upped one another on tours.

"Where are you from?"

"I'm from Cambridge," the euphemism for Harvard.

"Where are you from?"

"I'm from Providence," the euphemism for Brown.

"Where are you from?"

"I'm from New Haven," the euphemism for Yale.

"Where are you from?"

"I'm from *Harlem*," the euphemism for Columbia.

Those on the tour would pepper the house officer guides, who had applied and been accept the year before and were now leading tours, with the same questions week after week, questions asked coast to coast by prospective trainees.

"Do residents get to start their own IVs?"

"Do the attendings like to teach?"

"Can I get a good fellowship after training here?"

I remember one fellow from Georgetown medical school, who asked me, "Do you have an opera in town?"

"Yes, we do," I answered, adding, "What operas have you seen?"

"*Don Giovanni* and the other one whose name I forgot."

Boston had a splendid opera, and Dr. Peacock's wife was their chief administrator. Once she received a late Friday call that a troupe of conquistadors who were to perform that evening would be delayed, their travel arrangements disrupted by a major storm. Thirty in number, their absence would be a disaster, a travesty to catch the attention of the stern *Boston Globe* arts editor.

She made a phone call. That evening the program noted in the understudy section: "The Conquistadors will be played by Dr. Peacock and colleagues."

In act two the bony and white-legged physicians moved to the right and left in orderly procession, wooden pikes in hand. In spite of occasional bumps against the person to the right and to the left, overall the show went well. They even sang short choruses, mostly in pitch.

The next day the weary delayed troupe finally reached town. Dr. Peacock was disappointed to be relieved of his "starring" role. He later boasted that he and the other MDs received better reviews than the professional actors.

I too had a starring role in a production of *La Traviata*. A doctor's bag was needed for the scene where the heroine, dying of consumption, was visited by an apothecary. Who had a doctor's bag? I did—a gift from a drug-detail man in medical school.

I was given a row of tickets to watch my black-and-brass bag's debut. I shared tickets with residents and our dates, who relished such a treat.

My seat was behind a woman with a brown mink coat who sat high on a red rubber ring used by hemorrhoid sufferers. She arranged the doughnut mid-chair, taking five minutes in full.

The trial sit: "No, move it a bit to the right," she whispered.

Trial sit again: "Too far to the right; move it to the left," she said.

Trial sit again: "Now too far back."

Like a cat looking for a corner to curl and nap, she finally found her spot.

In act three the heroine—thin, pale, and elegant—was dying on a couch. The doctor walked in, a long black coat buttoned from below his knees to under his chin. In his right hand, beaming in the spotlight, was my bag!

I saw the image of my mother. "Son, we are so proud of you!"

Our row erupted in long, hand-painful applause, the vibrations knocking the rubber doughnut out of place. I no longer minded the repeat of the sit trials to follow; I had had my theatrical debut!

——◆——

The pediatric interviews were less formal than those of internal medicine and surgery. The agenda was a tour by a house officer, happy and smart, then two interviews by faculty. This was the only institution where they gave us our packet, our dossiers, to carry and present to our inquisitors.

I was curious to see what my medical school and references wrote about me, since we signed forms stating, "We waive all rights to read the good, bad, and untrue facts that you will write about us."

My interviewer was running late. Sitting on a wood bench in the hallway, looking right and left, I was alone. I looked right and left, and after confirming that I was alone, I opened the unsealed envelope and read the good and the inaccurate that were typed on letterhead stationery.

My interviewer appeared on cat feet, unheard by me in my trance of concentration.

"Anything interesting?" she said.

After a red-faced "oops," we spoke for an hour. A real dialogue, we discussed metabolic storage diseases, where proteins and other substances lodged in the brain, heart, muscles, and liver.

She next asked, "Where's your personal statement? I like to read these."

"I didn't write one," I said.

"Why not?" she asked.

"You have my record of four years. How can a silly contrived mass of words mean anything?" I answered.

"This is a first for me," she said followed by a pause. Then she continued, "You're right!"

Later, when my turn came to lead the "I really love this place" tours. I would read these statements of the applicants, categorizing them in several generic forms.

"I knew I wanted to be a doctor when, as a little girl, I saw Grandpa die of lymphoma."

Or, "While playing the cello in boarding school, I had an epiphany. My cello playing concentration would help make me a good physician."

Or, "I really want to help people, and I'm not interested in money. That's why I want a career in pediatrics."

What a contrast was my interview day at Man's Greatest Hospital to my crosstown interview at the hospital that called itself "Man's Greatest Children's Hospital," or *the* Children's Hospital of Boston. I was interviewed by a senior resident who talked for an hour, explaining why she didn't shave her legs, which was why she wore plaid knee socks. I pretended I cared, saying, "I don't shave my legs either and I *love* plaid socks!" But when she started to talk about her armpits, I stood, saying, "It's time for my next interview."

The gray-haired Chair across town, a brilliant physician, sounded like Julia Childs as she addressed us as a group. She crossed her hands over her stomach, playing with the buttons of her cardigan sweater. She wore a tight brooch on a choker necklace around her neck.

"Let me tell you why we *are* THE best," she started. When she was done twenty minutes later, I walked out, no tour wanted.

"Not for me," I muttered under my breath *wanting* to be heard.

Prey to the bad first impression, as I later worked with our crosstown resident rivals at Man's Greatest Children's Hospital, I looked back at my shortsightedness, better appreciating the greatness of that hospital and its marvelous physicians. But such was the crystalizing impression of the interview day.

How we were mixed and matched with our post–medical school home for training was at the hands of the "match system." They ranked us; we ranked them. Like dice being dropped out of a tin cup shaken by monkeys, our futures were set by the mix and the spill of our competitive lot.

Most times the mix worked well for us and the institution; sometimes it went badly for both. The program and the interns were so interdependent that if the fit was bad for one, it was worse for the other. When there was no win for either side, victims of a bad shake, arrangements had to be made to avoid midyear dropouts.

The problem children came in different styles, united by their universal lack of judgment and their inability to make decisions—sound or not. Expected to be independent in our day-to-day actions, we weren't watched by the Gray Hairs. We made our own decisions, ordered our own tests, and decided who needed surgery. There were no over-your-shoulder eyes to supervise, not even when we were exhausted with sleep debt.

One problem child was a resident who had flat brown hair flipped to the side. He had a straight black mustache that was only one inch wide—not a good look. He wore white starched pants, thick like stovepipes. Yet he couldn't make decisions. Dr. Bigelow once said, "Given an infinite amount of time, he would always make the right decision." With the paralysis of analysis, he couldn't act, incongruous with our pace of clinical needs.

We had another resident from Switzerland, whom we called "Swiss Miss." She was fluent in five languages, but in pressing situations, the five languages spoke to her in unison and nothing intelligible came out.

We had a resident from the Middle East. An oil company paid for her year with us, a "freebie" not to be sneered at. Coming from a hospital where she walked behind men and answered last, she had trouble being on the front line.

Discussions with the Chair, discussions with the chief residents, assignment of mentors—multiple actions were taken to mitigate the problem child. Seldom were these actions effective. You either had it or you didn't.

Another group of problem children were policed and guided by us, not the Gray Hairs. These were the house officers with good judgment but who were either ponderous or lazy.

One chubby resident simply did less work than the rest, choosing to pontificate on conditions that other residents were treating. During morning rounds, we'd sit and talk about the admissions of the day and he would just blab away. It finally stopped when a voice from the back yelled, "Are you here to lecture us, or did you just climb up here to lay your eggs?" We were social workers for one another. Sleep deprivation, unrealistic expectations, cancer, death; these travails took their toll on us, making personal relationships difficult.

One resident who went to Yale was perpetually having boy trouble. Her Yale legacy, we were told, was sleeping with the starting offensive line of the football team. She cried, "My boyfriend this. My boyfriend that."

And always the line of reassurance was the same. "Yes, this sucks."

The surgeons had problem children of a different sort. Their first love was the OR, and they sometimes eschewed the necessary work on the floors and the EW. These house officers were often nowhere to be found. Pages went unanswered and work was ignored, left for the surgeon of the next day to mop up. One neurosurgeon trainee failed to respond to EW pages for a patient who had a head bleed. Another orthopedic resident refused to answer a page to set a femur fracture, choosing to sleep in his call room with his beeper battery out.

Different from pediatrics, surgery supervision came from the more senior residents, not from the Gray Hairs. Thus, instead of the cardiac surgery rotation you wanted, you'd spend a month doing bowel preps. Instead of time on plastic surgery, you were assigned to podiatry at the VA hospital.

When the twelve-month clock of our intern year ticked down, we knew the problem children remedy was near. That remedy was a firm handshake of thanks and a ticket out of town—an unfortunate reflection of failure for both sides. And when the departures happened, I wondered if those who remained were indeed better suited for our hospital roles than those who left. Or perhaps, I reflected, we were also problem children who managed to fly just below radar of problem recognition, screened by the problem children above.

Wintertime

After a moose comes through your Subaru's windshield when you're driving sixty miles an hour on a snowy road in Maine and you're discovered unconscious with a thready pulse, there's hope—although not much. Man's Greatest Hospital would try to undo the inevitable.

"Winters in New England seldom look like the snowy days of Norman Rockwell paintings," Dr. Bigelow used to say. In these paintings we see a candle flickering in a window of a one-story house; there's snow on the roof, and wreaths with red bows hang on the door. Deer with heads bent eating junipers are there too. Winters in New England are often gray, and the snow is white only when it's new. The sun goes down at 4:00 p.m. and rises at 7:00 a.m. Months would pass before we'd see the sun at the bookends of our shift.

The Checkmark Surgeon was offered a weekend stint at Waterville Valley, a mountain resort in New Hampshire in exchange for manning first-aid stations for forty-eight-hour stints. Skiers with fractures and head injuries would be glided down icy slopes on toboggans by the Ski Patrol. The physician on hand would tend to the person at the station at the bottom of the hill—a small, square log building with a huge red cross on all sides.

Wags and I had never skied before, and a chance for a weekend in the mountains was fantastic. I was there with one of the Cathys. The Checkmark Surgeon was there with the intensive care unit nurse he later married.

Wags brought a rapturous toothpaste model with teeth like Chiclets. Following drinks, snacks, and meals, she would scoot into restrooms to brush her teeth. She didn't drink red wine, coffee, or anything that would stain her pearly whites. She ate colorless food rather than risk marring her livelihood. She skied wearing a mouth guard that was double the size of those worn by New England Patriots football players.

Ski lessons were basic, beginning on rolling slopes marked by green-circled signs. Slopes on the next higher tier were marked with blue squares. The black-diamond slopes were the most severe, with steep drops and six-foot moguls. One day of lessons complete, we graduated from the green to the blue slopes.

At the top of the mountain, chairlifts deposit skiers, who slide off the moving wooden benches and glide twenty feet down a short exit chute to make way for those disembarking next in fifteen-second intervals. For the novice, this hop-off isn't natural; for Wags it was impossible. He criss-crossed his skis as he jumped, landing him on his stomach. His falls were met with glares from the lift operators, who had to stop the lifts, leaving cold skiers swinging on benches fifty feet off the ground.

When the lift operators had their fill of Wags's difficult disembarkments, they no longer stopped the chairlift when he fell. Rather they dragged Wags by his boot bindings, filling his coat with snow and ice from the belly up along the way.

"*Stoooop!*" he would yell. "*Leave me alone.*"

There was no sympathy, and the more he screamed, the longer they dragged him.

Following a dinner of mashed potatoes, cauliflower, white bread, boiled chicken, and white wine, we sat in the bar lounge. I chatted with a guy wearing a black leather coat, not the typical bright parkas of skiing. "What do you do for a living?" I asked.

"I'm the biggest drug dealer in New England," he answered. That was no lie. The next year we saw him on the news after he was arrested at Logan Airport as he awaited the arrival of a drug mule on a flight from Central America.

The next morning, the Checkmark Surgeon was urgently summoned to the slopes while it was still dark. A member of the Ski Patrol was checking the ski runs, bounding over black-diamond run moguls until he went airborne and crashed into the side of snowcat grooming the trails. The Checkmark Surgeon found the man pulseless. Inspecting the severity of the skier's massive injuries, he called the coroner instead of the ambulance.

While the Checkmark Surgeon was putting a red coat over the ski patrolman's head in New Hampshire, the man who had hit a moose with his Subaru in Maine was being found by a snowplow operator clearing the roads. He radioed the accident to the highway maintenance dispatcher. The ambulance arrived thirty minutes later; EMTs stabilized the victim and called the Life Flight helicopter transport team.

We knew the Life Flight attendants, male and female nurses who had worked in our intensive care units and jumped at the opportunity to become part of the medical airborne. They dressed in tight, bright blue jumpsuits that resembled the slinky ski outfits of New England "snow bunnies." They transported patients intubated, inflating the lungs with squeezes of black rubber ventilation bags. They bagged their patients until their arrival in the EW or one of the surgical intensive care units.

After the helicopter landed on the hospital roof back in Boston, the driver, a young man, was sent to the EW, where massive brain swelling could be seen on the CT scan. He was moved upstairs to the surgical ICU with IV fluids running wide open; epinephrine and dopamine were infused to support his blood pressure. He was transfused throughout the night as his bowel and kidneys leaked blood.

Three hours later, his family arrived after a white-knuckle ride from Maine, driving as fast as possible in a New England storm in a noisy Ford pickup truck with tire chains. They arrived when the EEG showed no brain wave activity. The parents said their son had been honorably discharged from the Army six months earlier.

Wiping her eyes and her nose, his mother said, "I want to donate his organs." Her husband had his arm around the soldier's sixteen-year-old sister, who was weeping, not wailing—New England stoic.

The soldier shared the intensive care unit with others who were critically ill. There was a sixty-seven-year-old stockbroker whose aorta ruptured at work. He had been lucky enough to make it to the operating room, but the aortic rupture had taken its toll; he was now in kidney failure. A forty-five-year-old woman was in acute renal failure after having a near fatal-crash in suburban Newton. She taught at Brandeis University. A thirty-year-old woman was dying from liver failure. She had two children in diapers; her husband brought them in every other day for her to hug and kiss.

The doctors in the intensive care unit knew the patients' medical problems, but only the nurse knew the patients' personalities and their families. They stood by the grieving family as the covering physician was at the desk writing medication and fluid rate orders.

Physicians went from EW to floor, from EW to OR, from rounds to conferences during their workdays. Nurses, though, stayed in their units for entire shifts, with a short break for meals.

Nurses at many hospitals move right into ICU positions following graduation, often with slim experience. At Man's Greatest Hospital, though, securing a position on the units was the brass ring many nurses aimed for. Two or more years of floor experience were needed, and the recommendations from the floor charge nurses had to glow. Just as the applying surgeons were grilled, aspiring ICU nurses next sat for written exams. If they passed the tests, interviews were next. A group of nurses would ask rapid- fire questions.

"What's the antidote for a Coumadin overdose?"

"How do you calculate the rates for epinephrine infusions?"

"Look at this EKG. What's the arrhythmia?"

"Would you ever date an intern you work with every day?"

"What if he's engaged?"

Nursing shifts went from 7:00 a.m. to 3:00 p.m., from 3:00 p.m. to 11:00 p.m., or from 11:00 p.m. to 7:00 a.m. Some nurses with young families worked 7:00 p.m. to 7:00 a.m. two shifts a week to earn a full salary, allowing them to be home with their young children during the day. For those without children, a twelve-hour shift maximum meant their sleep debt came from nights of partying.

Nursing work was different from ours, but it mandated the same keen concentration and insights as the physicians. We appreciated that their jobs were tougher than ours in some aspects. Families and patients would ask question after question, which we didn't have time to answer. As the interns' work crescendoed, they'd page themselves away, leaving it to the nursing staff to translate the medical care and detail treatment plans to the families.

They were our eyes, our insight, and our hands on the floor. They looked for the patient about to "crump," the decompensating ill. They put shrouds over waxy faces after patients died. They calmed the patient the next bed over when the other patient in a shared room was coded and died. They knew to go over heads and call the Gray Hairs when we weren't doing our jobs. When we were pricks, we paid the price.

A recent nursing school graduate was concerned about a woman who had had her gallbladder removed earlier in the day. The woman had severe abdominal pain and was breathing quickly. The intern the nurse called blew her off, refusing to see the patient.

The charge nurse, who organized nursing assignments for the shift and supervised the floor, called next. The charge nurses were like our Gray Hairs, but they rose to positions of authority and respect at much younger ages than we could. And there was no gray hair in the bunch.

The senior nurse called, repeating the young nurse's concern, saying, "*Get here now.*"

Dismissive, the resident ignored her too.

She called again. "Do you know who this is?" she yelled into the handset.

"No," he said.

"*Good. Then eat shit!*" she said, slamming the handset.

An attending problem child caught the ire of the nursing staff too. A junior attending finished specialized training in repairing the defective hearts of children, graduating with a temper that exceeded his considerable skills. Explosive temperament was rare at Mass General, where humanity was in the air. This surgeon had learned only the technical aspects of his trade from his Gray Hairs, not their poise or professionalism.

He was in the pediatric ICU, looking at the chart of one of his post-operative patients and not liking what he read. His nostrils flared and he began to hyperventilate. He stood, grabbed the chart like a Frisbee, and threw it against a wall, pages fluttering to cover the linoleum floor. The mothers and fathers at the bedsides of their sick children stood too—and ran from the room.

"My patient would be safer in a New York City subway!" he yelled. Then he and his arrogance walked out the door.

That night, after finishing an operation, he headed to his red BMW convertible in a physician-only parking space. He looked down to see four flat tires. Then he noticed that the tire valve stems had been sliced. A red lipstick kiss was on the windshield.

The night we were amusing the New Hampshire drug dealer with hospital stories, the ICU nurses were stabilizing the moose victim: transfusing, infusing pressers, comforting the family members. The next morning the evening crew left at 7:00 a.m. Shivering in the dark and fifteen-degree parking garage, they started their cars and went home.

Some played with their infants for most of the day before taking a four-hour nap. At 7:00 p.m. they were driving back to the hospital in the dark and the cold, spotting fresh snow that made Boston look clean, and then they were back in the unit. When they returned that night, there were two empty beds—welcome relief, as assignments would be lighter.

At midnight, a woman was wheeled into the ICU, blood infusing through IVs in both arms; a large transverse incision on her abdomen was weeping blood. The surgical drains in her right side were dripping.

Removing the blue hair bonnet that the patient wore to the OR, they recognized the mother of two who had developed liver failure at the end of her second pregnancy. The nurses also recognized that this was the soldier's last gift.

Most times organ transplants are anonymous, and families flock to the hospital for the first time after the new organ is in place. Those needing organs are often at home dying of their diseases, some quickly and some slowly, waiting for their special beeper to sound. This is the beeper that says, "Your new life is here; get to the hospital ASAP."

Like they did with the soldier, the nurses transfused, gave fluids, and infused epinephrine and dopamine to the mother. Now there was a different family to comfort in a different way—the cries of mourning swapped for joyous cries of new life.

At 7:00 a.m. the nurses were heading through the hospital lobby into winter darkness, soon to be with infants at home, soon to get a bit of sleep before their next shift started.

This Monday morning, as they walked out to their cold cars, Wags and I were walking in from our black-diamond winter weekend. Stopping to chat in the parking lot, seeing our breath while hopping leg to leg to avoid shivering, we listened to their story of what the moose had ended and started. As they spoke, I reflected on the shame of the snowcat, not just for the loss of the skier but also for the loss of the others he could have saved.

And as the nurses drove home, they reflected on their weekend too. They saw the face of a dying soldier donor; they saw the face of the reborn young mother. They saw the faces of two different families who, in their different ways, wanted life to go on.

Meningitis Madness

Invasive infections hit different parts of the body—the skin, the ears, the lungs. Those hitting the brain, though, are the worst, vicious infections that could steal a child's bright future. Meningitis comes in many forms—viral, bacterial, and fungal—and the visages and consequences of each vary with the age of the infected. Before the development of vaccines to prevent this scourge, we were knee-deep in meningitis madness.

My first meningitis case, two months out of medical school, was an eight-week-old girl carried in by her young mother. Not feeding well for two days, she became listless. Her temperature was 102 degrees, and when she lay on the exam table, she followed my steps with her sunken eyes as much as she tracked her mother. As I pressed the soft spot on the top of her skull, she moaned and didn't cry.

She was placed on her side, and I performed a lumbar puncture. There were no objections from the young blond mother, who knew her daughter's future hung in balance. Inserting the needle, I was through the meninges, the sheath of the spinal cord, with a soft pop. The spinal fluid dripped; not mountain spring clear, it was lemonade cloudy.

On the cluttered microlab bench in the EW, I stained the spinal fluid and saw an ocean of bacteria dancing in blue pairs. After IVs were inserted and antibiotics were pushed in her veins, the baby girl was brought up to the sixth floor.

On the infant floor we had a meningitis room. It was deliberately located next to the nurses' station to permit close observation. As the babies panted, they were moaning, fluid restricted, and febrile. Located on the other flank of the nurses' station was the apnea, or SIDS, room—the room of the well.

Usually the infected children recovered. Some developed seizures; others developed trapped clusters of pus under the skull that the surgeons drained with dime-size burr holes. This baby had group B streptococcus as the offending pathogen, acquired during birth. The older infants, those of toddler age with just a few teeth, developed *Haemophilus influenzae*, or "H flu." Graciously, a pediatrician developed a vaccine to end this disease, starting his quest when the big drug companies showed no interest in developing a pediatric disease preventative, instead directing their scientists to find the next billion-dollar drug.

H flu was aggressive. It could infect the brain, the lungs, and the eyes. The epiglottis, which covers the trachea, would be infected too. Epiglottitis occurred, causing the tissue to swell to the size of a thumb, choking children. When H flu was suspected, kids went to the OR for emergency intubations. At times purple, these babies had their windpipes cut to insert breathing tubes.

We always had H flu children on the wards—crying and moaning, their parents crying and moaning along with them. We had protocols we followed. Each day we weighed the babies, measured the salts in their blood, and measured their head size. These babies remained febrile for a week or longer; then, just shy of the two weeks of intravenous antibiotics, the fever would break.

Two weeks of IV antibiotics was a long time to keep tiny Teflon catheters threaded in small veins. We stuck IVs everywhere—on top of the wrists, on the bottom of the wrists, on the feet, inside the elbows. We'd shave the scalp in patches, looking for blue veins. Though this was objectionable to parents, these veins were the easiest to hit.

Wags told me that sometimes he'd use the scalp veins of the old bald men he'd care for when he couldn't start an IV anywhere else. Seeing these, the gray-haired surgeons would say, "What the hell! Oh, you're the one who rooms with the pediatrician."

Some residents were better at IVs than others, blessed with great dexterity and X-ray vision to see the small coursing vessels like tiny Scotch pine needles. There were others who couldn't stick a needle in an orange sitting on a table.

Those with special skills, usually the junior or senior residents, were at the top of their game and never blinked when interns asked for help. Never were favors expected in return. They had needed help in the past and would in the future.

There were unusual forms of meningitis coming through the EW as well. One teenage boy was well known to us, having been regularly hospitalized with sarcoidosis that formed dime-size ulcers in his kidneys and lungs. To quell the inflammation, he was started on steroids and Imuran. This was a setup for weird bugs. He also had hepatitis B.

His father used to operate the big cranes on the Boston Harbor docks and unloaded steel containers from cargo ships. He worked just four hours a day for more than one hundred dollars an hour so that he could maintain his concentration with tens of thousands of dollars' worth of goods in those mobile steel sheds. For us in medicine, I wondered why there were no limits to the forty-eight-hour-plus shifts.

Under the green and rusty trestles of the Boston Garden, the teenager sold hot dogs to those going in and out of Celtics and Bruins games. Since he was a hepatitis carrier, we and he knew he shouldn't be doing this. Yet his desire to work beat out reason and trumped our finger wagging and admonitions of "You can't do this!"

Above where he parked his dented silver food cart, pigeons roosted. Some were gray and white, some piebald, some with shiny green breasts. Some were fat and healthy; others were scrawny, missing toes and eyes.

The birds would empty their cloacae onto mounds of droppings under their favorite roosts. They would hit pedestrians exiting the local T stop. I never understood why Chinese culture says you're lucky if hit with bird crap. If true, many folks were lucky; so was this boy.

Within the bird droppings lives the tiny fungus cryptococcus. It doesn't hurt the strong, only those with weakened immune systems. The fungus penetrates the brain by traveling through nasal passages.

The hot dog salesman came in on a hot afternoon with a stiff neck, squinting at the ceiling lights. He was flipped onto his side and a needle stuck in his back with a pop. Scanning his spinal fluid, we saw the big round bugs that stained black, looking like painted eggs. He stayed with us a month until the infection faded. Then he was back on Causeway Street, hawking his hot dogs and hepatitis.

We had other kids who would get weird brain infections that caused their eyes to pop out. Scuba divers got infections of their sinuses that oozed to the base of the brain, causing half the head blood vessels to clot. The blood-filled vessels behind their orbits pushed out their eyes. Other times eyes popped out when H Flu invaded the skin around the eyes and caused periorbital cellulitis. This too spread into the brain, causing meningitis.

Wags and I were busy midyear and were seldom home, and when we were home, we were off-sync. Our city-chasing times together became fewer. Our apartment was quiet. The mummy, now out of his glass case, stood neglected and was used as coat rack. The mice weren't around for nuisance company either. I think they died after ingesting the poisons in the bunting that wrapped the mummy's feet.

The parent of a child I treated gave me a gift certificate to a pet store—an unusual gift that I accepted graciously. Heading across the Charles to a pet store, I returned with a tuxedo-gray cockatiel named Aristotle.

Aristotle flew about our apartment, perching on curtain rods, kitchen handles, and the mummy. He too was neglected with our every-other or every-third-night call schedule.

After a forty-eight-hour call stretch, I came home to find Aristotle's eye protruding, mucous crystals clogging his pencil-tip nostrils. He was breathing fast. Did he have the disease of my scuba diving patients? Had periorbital cellulitis set in?

He couldn't turn his head side to side. Seeing my bird's stiff neck, I diagnosed avian meningitis. I took antibiotics from the ward and squirted chloramphenicol down his gullet. Just like how I did with kids, I adjusted his dose for his weight. He died the next day. I dropped him out our living room window onto the mouse carcasses that piled below, our own pet cemetery.

Neck stiffness is a herald of meningitis. You can't look up. You can't touch your chin to your chest. Your head hurts from the inside. The next building over, two surgeons shared an apartment. Just acquaintances, they shared cooking and cleaning chores. He was going into vascular surgery and had a Bill Murray–type personality. She was going into neurosurgery, where she would deal with the complications of meningitis and other brain infections. She drilled burr holes into heads and made skull flaps to allow pus to drain.

Hygiene on the Hill was a matter of convenience, and the neurosurgeon would cut the vascular surgeon's hair—quick scissor cuts, nothing fancy. This day he was less cooperative than usual, going to bed after his trim, no night out on a post-call evening.

The next day he was in the emergency room. Lumbar puncture done by a medical student, viral meningitis was diagnosed. The headache, the nuchal rigidity, and the fear of bright lights had been missed by the neurosurgeon barber the night earlier.

Doctors' children too became infected. One infectious disease attending, about ten years older than we were, had three-year-old twin girls. Camping in New Hampshire, they acquired echovirus meningitis. Lumbar punctures in tandem, diagnosis completed, their stay was shorter than the H flu babies.

One perplexing case came from St. Louis. The father, an expert in infectious diseases, had a high-achieving son thirteen years old. An A+ student and cross-country star, his father hoped that someday he would join our ranks at Man's Greatest Hospital.

At the start of eighth grade, the boy slipped into a coma. Lumbar puncture after lumbar puncture, nothing shined. Viral serology studies weren't revealing. He was seen at the Mayo Clinic and Johns Hopkins, the rivals of Man's Greatest Hospital. Diagnosis elusive, the boy had been on his back for six months; Man's Greatest Hospital was the last hope.

Transported by ambulance at great cost, the boy arrived with black curly hair, thin and pale. A nasogastric feeding tube was in his nose secured with thin pink plastic tape. The neurologists convened.

"Could this be von Economo's encephalitis lethargica?" the most senior member of the group asked. A lengthy discussion was held about von Economo's encephalitis lethargica, a disorder that was transiently reversible with dopamine-like drugs to substitute for a missing brain chemical.

Man's Greatest Hospital was systematic in approaching rare diseases. No assumptions made, wide nets were cast to look for clues. The neurologists ordered EEGs and brain imaging studies. He was seen by infectious disease specialists, who left with tubes of bloods and nasal swabs.

The child psychiatrists showed. One was minister-like, gray haired, peaceful in his speech; the other was stocky, with Popeye forearms. They asked the doctor father about his son, focusing on the time before coma onset. They ignored the fever and the sore throat the boy had the day before he lost consciousness.

The gentle psychiatrist grabbed the unconscious boy's arm. He held it over his face for a long minute waving it to be sure it was flaccid. Then he let go. Instead of hitting his nose with a clunk, as in true comas, the falling arm drifted away from the boy's face, falling to the pillow by his ear like a drifting feather.

No meningitis madness, no stroke, no von Economo's encephalitis lethargic; the boy had a "conversion reaction." Too stressed in early teenage years, wanting to escape from the pressures of life, unconsciously his mind had shut down in coma-like sleep. The neurology team assembled, and the case of the boy from St. Louis was reviewed. The Gray Hairs spoke.

"Physical therapy! Physical therapy! Physical therapy!"

"Get this boy up and moving."

"No more tests. No more labs."

"No more parental pushing!"

"Tell the doctor he has to calm down if he ever wants to see his son's eyes open again!"

The genius of Man's Greatest Hospital had struck. The boy went home, and the mysterious brain infection was over.

The real infections would return soon. A boy five years old came to the EW with a temperature of 104 degrees, spots head to toe, and low blood pressure. Meningococcal meningitis, a high-mortality disease, was diagnosed. Intravenous antibiotics, fluids, and hydrocortisone were pushed. The boy was lucky to survive.

In came a sixteen-year-old girl with the same presentation as the boy—high fever, spots, shocky. This time the shock was permanent; she died.

Those exposed to these patients could meet similar fates, since the bugs were spread by air, taking microscopic trips on air drafts. We were prescribed the antibiotic rifampin so that we'd be spared. Rifampin has a funny quality—it's orange and bestows its bright glow on the taker. On this medicine, you'd blow your nose to find the tissue orange. You'd cry and see bright yellow tears. You'd urinate and the toilet water would turn highway-cone orange.

The wave of meningococcal meningitis subsided. But like the white contrails of jets in the high blue sky, the orange trail of meningitis madness followed us. Orange-tinged tissues filled trash cans. Drops of orange urine stained the bathroom floor. Orange drops were on toilet seats.

After needle sticks, the prophylactic drugs we took left no visible trails to mark our exposure. The only signs were wrinkled brows that relaxed only after months of negative blood test results. Now, like highway flags, the orange trails waved a warning about our job risk.

Taking rifampin, sitting alone at the evening meal to ponder for a while, I wondered who among us would be infected. Who among us would die from the diseases of our occupation?

Surprise Me

When the daylight shortens and the long cold Boston winter sets in, days drag. With no Sox games and no beach time, dealing with meningitis sprinkled with shock and death, house officers became pale, and some became sullen. Work became robotic as Wags and I glided our way around the floors, comfortable caring for the diseases we diagnosed. Nights at bars were punctuated by cold blasts when we stepped outside to shiver our way back home.

Like spots on a child erupting with chickenpox, parties would break out from boredom. These events varied from large to small, but usually twenty guests was the norm. Some had themes; most didn't. When it was our turn to host, we settled on a "Surprise Me" party, with items to be presented for the amusement of others.

Loud events in high-rise buildings are usually greeted by knocks at the door and a parade of complaining neighbors.

"Can you keep it down?"

"My mother is visiting from Kansas and needs her sleep."

"My wife is trying to conceive, and your noise is disrupting her fallopian tube flow."

The police would come if you pushed too far. Because we patched and splinted them, helping them after crashes and other traumas, they had a fondness for us. When they arrived, no citations were given, just plain words of "Try to keep it down" were spoken, followed by "How late will you be going? We're off at midnight. Can we stop over?"

Police respect of medical personnel was usually solid, though not always. They were fonder of the nurses than us. A resident in emergency medicine who was rotating for a month at a hospital in Worcester, about sixty miles west of Boston, was on his way to the hospital for his shift. He drove an ugly Datsun B-210, green with gray duct tape holding in the taillight lens. He was pulled over.

"License and registration please," said the patrolman.

The resident put his hospital identification badge on top of his license, which was usually a free pass, except this time. The night before, a cop had been brought into the resident's emergency room. Not fast tracked, the police officer had to sit in a waiting room with drunks and coughers. This mistreatment had been discussed during the officer's morning roll call.

The police officer walked around the Datsun.

"You have one taillight out.

"You have an exhaust system leak.

"You have a cracked windshield.

"Your registration is expired.

"Your front turn signal light is out."

So went the car inventory.

"Please step out of the vehicle, sir," He said leaving out the *doctor* salutation.

"Your car isn't drivable and will be impounded."

It took an hour for the wrecker to come. And as his car was about to be hauled, the resident asked the cop, "Can I have a ride? I'm late for my shift?"

"Does this look like a cab?" barked the cop.

The resident walked to the hospital, two hours late for his shift. As he arrived, he was muttering weird phrases others strained to understand.

When his court date came, he said little before the judge, while the uniformed cop read the list of ten citations. The judge peered over the top of his reading glasses as the officer spoke. Then the judgment was rendered. "Stop bullying this fellow! Apologize to the young doctor," the judge admonished.

The judge continued, "It is good to see you again, *Doctor.*" The week before, the resident had cared for the judge's wife.

Around the same time, I was pulled over by Boston police after a rolling stop as I was getting onto the Charles River Bridge. The officer took my license and registration, and of course I handed him my hospital ID badge with the packet.

"I can cite you for not having a Massachusetts license, for not having your vehicle registered in town, and for having an out-of-state car insurance card.

"There's also the matter of the rolling stop.

"This will cost you about seven hundred dollars.

"However, I'm just going to give you a warning.

"*Doctor*, take care of yourself. Please attend to these matters."

Medical parties were special. On Halloween they were held on the top floor near the room where the page operators sat. Most costumes were lame, with medical themes. Wearing white long underwear with a white swim cap, Wags dressed year after year as a sperm. Curvy nurses dressed as cats in tight black suits. I'd cut holes for arms and legs in garment bags and go as a suitcase, underwear hanging from pockets. One year I went as the Stay Puft Marshmallow Man of *Ghostbusters* fame. I covered my arms, trunk, and legs with Marshmallow Fluff that took weeks to remove.

On Saint Patrick's Day, a surgical floor secretary would brew a special punch served in demitasse cups. The secret ingredient was methylene blue, of my blue toes fame, which after being consumed went out in the urine. Combine blue dye combined with yellow urine, and the result was a delightful green flow. In deliberate acts, toilets spanning the hospital went unflushed that day.

During the winter holidays, fancy events were sponsored by the surgeons, while modest gatherings were sponsored by other departments. To the envy of the other staff, at the top of the nursing pecking order were the nurses in the cardiac surgery ICU. They received pearl necklaces one year, gold bracelets the next. The rest of us received cards.

"Why buy expensive dresses for onetime use?" the young nurses would ask. The nurses of Man's Greatest Hospital were as crafty as they were smart. They would shop at Filene's and Jordan Marsh and not remove price tags, which they discreetly tucked inside or covered with matching Mystik tape. Parties over, the dresses were returned for a full refund, no rental costs incurred. Soon retailers became wise and affixed huge orange discs on apparel, which if removed voided refunds.

At the end of the year, we'd have "change parties," where the house staff switched. Sponsored by the departments, the senior residents would graduate with recognition and applause. Our change parties were held in the ballroom atop the Holiday Inn close to the hospital. On-call residents would sneak over with beepers on, ready to sprint back to the wards if STAT-paged. The nursing staff was trapped on the ward; they wanted to sneak over too, but that was impossible considering their hands-on duties.

On call for one change party, I snuck over to the party. Back at the hospital, all I wanted to do was sleep, as I had no ward work that night. Yet I was paged every thirty minutes. It was the nurses' form of discipline and rebuke.

There were indeed limits of conduct among house officers. At parties, none smoked. Sordid smoking-related disease was in our face day in and day out. At a time Boston was swarming with cocaine, we never saw white powder used. No smells of pot either. Just beer and cheap wine bought at the liquor store on Charles Street. We liked that store; they had a two-dollar bottle wine area—the "sleazy wine section," I called it.

At our party, the surprise was the mummy, draped in hospital linen, standing at attention in the corner near the window from where we dropped our snared mice. Some guests brought surprises, but most didn't. Surgeons came, nurses too. Most of the pediatric residents stayed home for quiet married dinners, but a few showed.

A "party leg" appeared—a prosthetic leg brought by a resident was stood in the corner. The hollow top of the plastic leg was wide enough to be a perfect fit for a wine bottle and ice.

Someone brought a fake hand in a jar of formaldehyde that looked real. It was a replica of a man's hand—light green and fat, with bulbous fingers and hairy knuckles that floated in the jar.

A long thin white bone, three feet long, was placed on the table by the chips.

"What's this?" asked one of the ladies. "This is weird."

"It's a whale's penis bone," said the proud owner.

She put the bone down saying, "Woof!"

A female resident went around feeling our hands and our biceps. She had begun to date a Boston Bruins defenseman, who she bragged was built like a boulder. None of us compared to his stony physique.

One of the surgeon-chasing floor nurses was there. On Friday night happy hours at the bar across the street from the hospital, she'd slip off her shoes to massage the crotch of the surgeon whose pants I had filled with ultrasound goop. She did this knowing he was in a steady relationship. But the resident was at the party with his new fiancée. And when the surgeon-chaser began toeing him when his fiancée was in the bathroom, he quickly left.

Like the countdown to New Year's Eve, the unveiling of Padihershef happened at midnight. As we took our guests' coats off the covered object in the corner, we next pulled off the white hospital bedsheet, exposing our friend. To our disappointment, they were more repulsed by the smell of the stale bunting than fascinated by the Egyptian artifact. "You put my coat on *that*!" yelled more than one woman.

Not much to see, just stationary gauze, none of our guests exhibited the fascination of Wags's patient in purple leather. Our only hope for some sort of mummy salvation was a call from the possible-Prince, since he was again in town for a show. Our driving reason for keeping the mummy so long was the long-shot hope that Wags's patient really had been Prince and would return for a private visit, but neither a visit nor a phone call came.

We were lucky that the mummy's disappearance hadn't been discovered. We were surprised that the gentleman who pushed his broom around the mummy's feet for years hadn't noticed the empty spot on the floor.

A month later, though, he came up to us and said, "Thanks for the referral. Now that I got my cataracts fixed, I can really see!" He continued, "Get some sun. You guys look wicked pale."

We feared that hospital talk of the party leg, the hand in the jar, and the whale penis bone would explode to conversation about the mummy. We knew that even with promises of "I won't say a word about your mummy," there would soon be talk of the mummy in the EW, ORs, wards, and bars.

As the crowd thinned at 2:00 a.m., we counted our blessing that the cops didn't return to party. Only three or four men and women remained, sipping drinks and laughing, the last chance to hook up for the night.

As we were throwing out half-empty beer cans and full glasses of cheap wine, we admitted to each other that the mummy had to go back *that night.*

The return of the mummy took place at 3:00 a.m., before the bakers were making their runs, before the squat green *Boston Globe* delivery trucks began dropping their bundles in front of drug stores. No planning involved, we put him back in his glass case, which we covered with a sheet. We then wheeled him to the elevator, took a ride down to the first floor, and rolled him across the street. We knocked on the back door, startling the security guard, who we caught in a head-down nap.

Wiping his eyes, he stood to let us in. "We're just returning something," said Wags. "OK," said the guard before going back to sleep.

We placed the mummy where he had stood for a hundred years and more to stand there again, having his feet hit by bristle brooms late in the night for a hundred years more.

Too tired to speak more than a few phrases on our quick walk home, we spoke of our disappointment in our guests. "How could they be more surprised by a whale's monstrous penis bone than by a two-thousand-year-old mummy," asked Wags. I answered, "Surprise lies in the eyes of the beholder."

Soon after we were back in our apartment and Wags had turned in, there was a knock at the door. Still awake, I opened the door.

It was Nikki, the over-tanned, oversexed nurse. "I just heard from the girls you're having a party. I want to see your mummy," she said, unzipping her coat and inching toward me.

"Wags," I yelled. "It's for you!"

As Wags came from his room, I heard him mutter, "Where's Prince when you really need him?"

PCP and CPC

He yanked a mounted Boston police officer off his horse on Boston Common. The accompanying officer, still on his steed, pulled a black baton from his utility belt and whacked the teen twice, once in the back and again on the shoulder, breaking the boy's collarbone. He jumped off his horse and pounced on the teen, handcuffing him in one quick motion.

Only one ambulance was called; it was for the teen. The officer who had been pulled from his horse wiped the dirt from his uniform and grumbled, "What is that kid on?"

A mile away in the EW, we were attending to a fourteen-year-old boy who was acting bizarrely at home. His mother called the Newton Police, who chased the boy, who bounced from room to room before being subdued and cuffed.

Brought to the EW by ambulance, his pulse was 140 beats per minute; the pupils of his eyes were wide and black, like a cat's at night. As he was rolled from the ambulance into the emergency room bay, the triage nurse asked, "What's that kid on?"

Uncuffed, the boy from Newton was in an exam room; security guards stood outside, ready to put the boy in locked leather restraints if we were judged to be in danger.

"What's your name?" I asked.

"What's your name?" the boy repeated in the time I spoke one word.

"Where are you from?" I asked.

"Where are you from?" came the telegraphed repeat.

"What did you take?" I asked.

"What did you take? What did you take? What did you take?" he said. As he repeated the questions, his pupils dilated and constricted like that of a parrot when you hold a peanut in front of its beak.

"Follow my finger," I said, moving my index finger in front of his face for his eyes to follow. He snapped at my finger, darting his neck forward with lips rolled back. The security guard pushed me back.

"That's it, Doc; no more."

He pressed his shoulder microphone, and two other security guards were soon at the bedside. They others pinned the boy on his back, pushing his head into the black rubber mattress. Locked leather restraints were affixed to each extremity.

"Doc, these kids on PCP try to bite you, you know.

"You betta learn to watch your fingahs!"

With security present, we drew blood for serum chemistries and toxicology, a "tox screen," to look for drugs and other chemicals in his circulation. We gave him ten milligrams of haloperidol, enough to keep him quiet for ten hours. The tox screen came back one hour later, positive for phencyclidine, PCP, the designer drug known as "angel dust."

"I don't know where he could have gotten it," said his weeping mother.

At least she admitted the raging boy was her son. Commonly parents said, "No, that can't be my boy." Other times they grimaced. "How would you like to take him home with you? *You* live with him. I'll throw in food for a year."

Drugs and teens, alcohol and teens, sex and teens, or combinations thereof were the multiple-choice questions of teenage life. Like the dreaded "K-questions" on our exams—A+C or B+D, all of the above or none of the above—when asked about their children, parents would answer "none of the above."

Kids weren't unique in buying drugs; purchases made with their fifty dollars, a week's allowance, or with twenty-dollar bills snuck from their parents' wallets. Young parents, those with babies in diapers, also spent their little money on cocaine, a drug said to addict instantly.

During a primary care rotation in Charlestown, I asked young mothers what they did for their careers.

"I'm in rehab for cocaine."

I asked the next mother I saw, "Do you work out of the house?"

"I'm in rehab for cocaine."

Such were the admissions of these skinny, pasty mothers, who spent more on cocaine than they did on diapers and formula. Thus we'd dispense diapers and free formula along with vaccinations.

Some of their kids were "toilet bowl babies." Teen pregnancies were hidden by loose fitting sweatshirts. After a night of drugs or drinking, premature labor started. At first the contractions were mistaken for gas pains; as the girl sat on the toilet, a blood-covered premature infant would drop out in a splash.

"Ma! Ma!" the girl would yell.

Five minutes later, an ambulance was there. Neighbors on stoops stood gawking. Ten minutes later, the infants were being cleaned, warmed, and given oxygen and antibiotics in the neonatal intensive care unit, saved from the sewer. We had trouble sympathizing with these mothers.

The boy with the fractured clavicle was now in an EW bay. The two mounted policemen stood at the exam room door, ready to knock him down again if he tried to escape.

"Not sure what he took, Doc," one of the officers said.

Sweating, holding his left shoulder where the baton had hit, the boy looked dazed, his pulse high and pupils large.

"What's your name?" I said.

"It's R...R...R...R...R...Rob," he said, stretching it over thirty seconds, as though he wasn't sure of it.

"Where are you from?"

"I...'...m f...r...o...m—" he said over another thirty seconds, the sentence drifting off incompletely.

His arm out, he cooperated when we drew blood as sweat dotted his brow. Blood was obtained for chemistry studies and a tox screen.

Dr. Yogur was walking through the EW and stopped at the pediatric desks to see if there were interesting cases for his medical students. He recognized the name of the boy with the clavicle fracture.

"I know this boy's brother," Dr. Yogur said. "I saw the brother with Dr. Peacock. The brother had Zollinger-Ellison syndrome."

Dr. Yogur was as fine a clinician as any of the Gray Hairs. He asked to examine the boy, parting his way between the two police officers. One officer recognized him from late-night calls to Yogur's salsa parties. Complaints were called in by his neighbor, who only wore her hearing aids when Dr. Yogur had guests.

"Hi, Doc. How's ya neighbah?" asked the patrolman.

Dr. Yogur looked at the sweating boy. Pivoting, he turned out of the room and found me. "Listen," he said, "this is not PCP. This boy has hypoglycemia. What's his glucose?"

I explained that the chemistry results weren't back.

"Get him some orange juice." Dr. Yogur then held the boy's head while helping him drink four ounces of orange juice. The boy awakened.

"Hey, I know you. You're Dr. Yogur," said the boy. "Where am I? My shoulder kills."

Dr. Yogur called the main chemistry laboratory.

"This is Dr. Yogur. I'd like to add an insulin level check to the blood sample."

"Doc," said the policeman, "you mean this kid isn't on drugs?"

"No." Dr. Yogur replied. "He has a tumor that's making excess insulin."

How could he know this? I thought. A brilliant diagnosis made in five minutes?

The next week, the boy went to the OR and had a mass removed from his pancreas. But this tumor was different. It was shaped like a fork, with a big central mass and fronds of insulin-producing cells extending out. Dr. Yogur named the tumor a "forkhead insulinoma."

The forkhead insulinoma was the hospital's first, I imagined. At Man's Greatest Hospital, cases that were the rarest of the rare, the bizarrest of the bizarre, were selected to be presented at legendary clinicopathologic conferences, or CPCs. After presentation, the case discussions are published in *The New England Journal of Medicine*, medicine's most prestigious medical journal. *Would the forkhead insulinoma make the cut?* I wondered.

Three weeks later, after the gray-haired pathologists met, the tumor was selected for a CPC! I would present the case as an unknown, dropping muted important clues in the midst of a formal presentation. An expert from another institution, a top clinician in the field, would dissect the case, announcing his clinical diagnosis at the end, hoping to avoid the embarrassment of getting it wrong.

How could anyone know about a forkhead insulinoma? I thought. This was a Mass General first. This is where great diagnoses go out; they don't come in.

The discussant, from the University of Pennsylvania, was the world's expert in hypoglycemia in children. Thoughtful, deliberative, he detailed what it could and couldn't be. He looked at X-rays, he listed the lab results, he commented on the tox screen. Then, like the scene in *The Ten Commandments* when Charlton Heston comes down from Mount Sinai with the stone tablets in hand, the discussant's revelation came.

"My diagnosis is, my diagnosis is," the suspense was building, "my diagnosis is *an insulinoma!*"

The audience burst into applause. A few of the endocrinologists stood when they clapped. I heard a few "hurrahs" too.

I was sitting next to Dr. Peacock, who never liked to be one-upped. He smiled as he turned to me and said, "He missed the forkhead."

This was the first time my name was in Man's Greatest Journal— *NEJM*, a prized case report from Man's Greatest Hospital. The pride exceeded what I had felt when my doctor's bag was in *La Traviata*.

In a sea of complex cases, as though smitten by the sirens' song, the seduction to discover new and rare diseases hit us. Each week we read the CPCs, learning to untie medicine's complicated knots. Reading these cases, we saw how the physicians in the audience were acknowledged. There would be single line in the *New England Journal of Medicine* that read, "A physician asked." But the pathologists soon learned our names, and when we asked our questions, our names were published in black and white. Our names were now in the published registry of Man's Greatest Hospital's great cases.

Such recognition meant more to me than any of the pathologists could conceive. As a medical student, with a state school inferiority complex before heading to Boston to compete with stars from Harvard, I devoured these cases. I read the CPCs, going back four years in full, looking for the common themes of diagnosis. I developed mnemonics for diagnostic algorithms. I constructed word strings of all known diseases I expected to see. I learned there were more weird and rare diseases than I imagined, and I hoped to one day to find the weird disease that would bear my mark.

With Dr. Peacock's help, I later presented the case of the young boy with the bump in the middle of his forehead. I presented the boy with the pillowy cheeks who was making mysterious hormones. Others in my group presented the girl with herpes meningitis.

We presented a five-year-old girl with Down syndrome who had a hole in her heart that resulted in extra blood flow her lungs. When she contracted influenza, all the blood vessels in her lungs clotted, something we learned at her autopsy.

There was a sixteen-year-old girl from Chelsea. Sick with a virus, she collapsed at home. Her parents found her when they came home from working in a supermarket. Tan in midwinter due to adrenal failure, she died of a simple infection.

There was a twelve-year-old girl with diabetes who failed to take her insulin, despite Dr. Peacock's kind pleas. She developed a fungus in her lungs, mucormycosis, which we knew targeted blood vessels. The surgeons debated what to do, operate or observe? She awakened at 2:00 a.m., sat up, and coughed; blood gushed from her mouth. Her autopsy showed that the fungus had eroded major blood vessels in her lungs.

But if you believed that the parents of the CPC children found solace in thinking that what we learned from their children would help others, you were wrong. One hundred–fold more tissues were used to wipe away tears than the number of CPC pages printed.

With all that we saw in medicine day and night, we learned more from the unusual and sad things than what did from the routine. Was this unconscious reality what made us focus on the weird and the rare? Did we publish cases of the weird and the rare so that others could learn, or did we want our names recorded for future generations to see how we struggled with the weird and the rare?

The answer to these questions was a bit of both.

What They Do to Each Other

Growing up in a calm suburban town, I didn't have much exposure to person-on-person brutality. My first look into the world of the horrific things people do to one another came after I saw a Salvadoran man's head bivalved with a machete by his wife in Chelsea.

A melting pot city, Chelsea was where Russians new to the United States were relocated by the government. It was here the "boat people" from Vietnam had their first start in this country. Chelsea was where refugees from the war in El Salvador, the war that Oliver North proudly defended before Congress, came. It was a city of diversity, with residents planting caring seeds for the next generations.

Part of our training involved working as pediatricians. We didn't work in the wealthy communities near Boston—Newton, Weston, or Wesley. We worked where there was poverty. The Chelsea Health Center was a redbrick building on top of one of the city's hills. The devoted staff worked there for years without turnover. The reception area was manned by Beth, close to sixty-five, a warm grandmother-type woman who knew the children in the waiting room by first name.

On my first day there, a mother brought her three-year-old daughter to see me. "Doctor, she fell out a window." The mother was crying, but the girl was fine. Falling out a back window four floors up, the girl had landed on ripped couch cushions on the sidewalk that were waiting for the next day's trash haul. Following a small bounce, the crying girl ran around the front of the apartment building to ring the doorbell.

Parent pride and respect shined there. Families earned minimum wage or less, being taken advantage of by those who hired new immigrants. Yet their children came for visits as though dressed for Easter. Girls wore ruffled and velvet dresses. The boys wore bow ties and shiny shoes. They brought gifts; some bought tiny ashtrays of wood saying "Guatemaltaca" or "El Salvadore." With singles and coins they paid the fifteen-dollar fee to have their daughters' ears pierced. They wanted their children to grow up to be doctors and lawyers, not wash and sand floors or stock shelves as they did.

One immigrant family, struggling more than most, lived at the base of the hill below the center. The husband sanded floors for a living; his wife worked as a cashier and was paid under the table. The health center took care of their kids.

An argument erupted, and the neighbors called the police. As the cruisers arrived, lights and sirens sounding, she swung a two-foot-long machete at her husband, landing it outside his right eye. The blade cut deeply, and the right third of his head wagged out, held on by a skin flap in the back.

Arriving to screams, the police officers powered their way through the front door and saw the side of the man's head swung out. They closed the head and called an ambulance. "*Get here fast!*" they screamed into their shoulder microphones as they kneeled in blood.

Five minutes later, the husband was in the EW. His wife was in jail. One hour later the man was in the OR. The slice missed his eye; only the outside part of his brain was sliced off. Two months later he was back to sanding floors with the gruesome scar of "Clam Man." He now raised his children alone. His wife was incarcerated for five years; he forgivingly visited her every weekend, bringing the children too.

During my training, I also witnessed the sordid transgressions of adults against children. One girl I cared for after a sexual assault was fourteen years old. She came in with her twenty-eight-year-old boyfriend— a skinny man with greasy, slicked-back hair. I called Social Services to notify them of a statutory rape.

Knowing that Social Services had been alerted, she skipped her scheduled appointments and, when ill, kept her distance. Three months later she was in the waiting room, this time alone, unable to control her arms, which writhed like crawling snakes. Her speech was slurred. I recognized the signs of Sydenham's chorea, a complication of untreated strep throat infections.

Six months later she came in pregnant. The twenty-eight-year-old boyfriend was the father. Social service agencies were contacted again. Now that she was pregnant, the safety net wasn't as strong. She was an emancipated minor who could make decisions independent of parents.

A plan was developed by the social workers. The next time the man and teen mother showed in the clinic, we'd stall them, alert the Chelsea police, and have the boyfriend arrested. Four months pregnant, she was back in my office—the delay was on. The boyfriend suspected a sting and started yelling, "You messing with me, Doc?" He pulled a six-inch switchblade from his back pocket.

I jumped up, threw a chart at him, gave him a rugby tackle that put him on the floor, and then ran down the hallway yelling, "*Beth, call the police!*" He left out the back door.

After that evening, I was walked to my car by Security. I constantly glanced right and left when I left that center until my car door locks clicked. The boyfriend was arrested and sentenced to only thirty days in jail for pulling his knife on a physician. The girl had the baby, and the chorea persisted.

That wasn't my lone involvement with the police. A six-year-old girl was brought in by her mother, who said, "She just ain't right."

She appeared fine and talked like a six-year-old should—nothing unusual in her affect, nothing unusual on physical inspection. With these sixth-sense cases, we swabbed the groin for bacteria. The next day the culture grew for gonorrhea, the lone clue of sexual abuse.

The mother's boyfriend was arrested, convicted, and sentenced to three years in jail. As the incarceration period ended, the district attorney called me in the midst of morning rounds on the pediatric wards. "The boyfriend gets out of jail tomorrow. He said he's coming after you."

Another case of abuse and another threat to me soon followed. A young boy came in bruised, with welts on his face and arms. He had large handprints on his chest and back too. Photos were taken of the injuries, and the police and Social Services were called. The mother's boyfriend was sentenced to two years in jail.

When the two years were up, I received another call from the district attorney regarding the imminent release.

"Just to alert you, the child beater gets out tomorrow. He said he's coming after you."

We defended children against abuse, and it was clear that the abusers weren't learning their lessons in the penitentiary. Rather, anger brewed, directed against those who acted as the guardians of children.

Receiving these threats, we alerted hospital security.

"We'll watch out for you, Doc," said the guards. "Stay close to home."

For months after the criminals were paroled, I watched my back. No nights out alone; never the same path home. No phone calls were answered at home, to the dismay of the Cathys, and we had our phone number unlisted.

Was this what I signed up for? I asked myself.

At times the sordid mixed with the comical, though. Two boys, five-year-old cousins, were brought in by ambulance. They had had a contest to see who would bite the other's penis the hardest. One turn, one chomp. The boy who was to go second came in with his phallus so severely bitten that just a small patch of skin remained on the base, barely enough for blood supply to help the postoperative healing. After surgery, the red-faced mothers laughed.

We cared for some patients up to twenty-one years old. Although eighteen years was the pediatric cutoff, we also saw many college students. The pediatric age cutoff was something that the fleas abused.

Syndromes, chromosomal abnormalities, and birth defects were the language of pediatrics, not the comfort zone for internists. I was paged to the EW by a medical resident and directed to one of the internal medicine bays. There lay a fifty-year-old woman with Down syndrome who looked like she was one hundred.

"She's yours. She has Down," said the resident.

I walked away, saying, "Do your job." I wanted the internists to give the genetically challenged the same respect we did, something I had learned from my mother when young.

A freshman college student, home for the summer, came in at 2:00 a.m. He was from Weston and told his story.

"I heard a noise in the backyard and went out. Two men held me down and shoved a one-liter Pepsi bottle up my ass."

We tried to get the bottle out. The bottom of the bottle had gone in first, so I tried pulling with my finger inside the bottle's mouth. No luck, so off to the operating room the fellow went. While he was under anesthesia, we told his parents, "Let your son stick with his story." Bottle removed, it was dropped into a recycling container in the hallway outside OR3.

Other weird objects were put into bodies, and we learned never to perform rectal exams on prisoners. The inmates in the jail around the corner tried many creative stunts to land a hospital vacation.

A high wall ringed the prison yard that bordered the main hospital entrance road; rusty razor wire was on the top. In front of the jail, at a fast-food stand, prison guards rested shotguns on their legs as they sat on picnic tables.

Jumping over the back wall, a prisoner escaped one midmorning in May. It was a twenty-foot drop over the wall to hospital property, and he was injured when he landed. Limping when he stood, he began to hobble away.

"Wham!" He was slammed to the ground—tackled by an ear, nose, and throat surgeon who was later dubbed "Chuck Norris."

In fact, several of the surgeons were sports stars, with football leading the pack. When Man's Greatest Hospital wanted to move into sports medicine, it accepted six members of the Stanford football team, strong, handsome, and pleasant fellows. Their destiny was orthopedic surgery and half-million-dollar-a-year-plus incomes.

The more severe the problem, the longer the convicts would stay. A guard outside the door was fine with them; hospital accommodations were better than jail. They learned to tell us that they were alcoholics and would have the DTs if not treated. They knew we had our own brand of whisky—Jack Daniels–shaped bottles with labels saying Man's Greatest Hospital's Whisky. The convicts would eat stones, metal shavings, and can openers with the intention of making their stomachs and intestines bleed. Some prisoners wrapped light bulbs with electrical tape and then swallowed them whole, like pythons swallowing whole rats. X-rays of abdomens looked like toolboxes.

You never put a hand in the mouth or the rectum of a convict for fear of puncture wounds. These risks were compounded, as several convicts had hepatitis or HIV. Even when they knew they were infected, they wouldn't tell you. If you pricked your finger with a needle used on them or you cut yourself on a sharp shard in their body, they wouldn't let you test them for hepatitis or HIV.

Surgery was usually needed; endoscopy and colonoscopy couldn't retrieve the junk box they had swallowed. If Wags assisted in these cases, I asked him the felon's names to see if any were the pedophiles I'd helped send away.

Wags also cared for drug mules. Brought in from Logan Airport by customs agents, these shackled individuals were short Hispanic men and women who peeked around nervously; none spoke English. They were led by their chains to the X-ray department.

Cocaine-packed condoms shaped like tiny sausages could be seen on radiographs. Some carried four, some ten; the most we counted on an X-ray was twenty-three. Usually the packets passed through the bowels unimpeded. Some packages, though, got caught in intestinal sphincters, leading to midflight vomiting. If the packages contained air, they would expand at high altitudes, causing in-flight misery. When passengers became ill in flight, the pilots alerted customs agents and the passengers were met by EMTs and police as soon as they stepped off the jetways.

Self-inflicted pediatric injuries were less common than those inflicted by others, but self-inflicted wounds did find their way to our wards. Girls with anorexia nervosa would starve themselves, vomiting meals and sneaking laxatives. Evading their parents, they hid their bony frames with loose clothing, as parents hid from the problems growing in their shrinking child. The girls would collapse at home or school. Sometimes a teacher, friend, or coach would sound the clarion call. Starved, these girls had low temperatures and pulses lower than marathon runners; salts in the blood were grossly disturbed.

As a world expert in metabolic disturbances, Dr. Peacock was consulted when these girls arrived. He'd say, "Don't bargain with them! Take away their clothes. If they take a thousand calories a day, they'll get their underwear back. If they don't take their food, we'll drop a tube and feed them!"

As a group, pediatricians are gentle souls, caring for those too young to speak for themselves, those too young to know what's in their best interest. Not surprisingly, some house officers were against Dr. Peacock's tough-love approach. They would sneak the girls their underwear. Residents would sit at the end of the bed twirling the patient's hair, pleading softly, "Won't you take a little sip pleeeeease?"

"Okay, I'll try," the manipulative teens would answer.

A teaspoon was swallowed in full manipulation.

"See? I told you I'd do it. Can I go home now?"

The more the patients and residents pleaded for leniency, the more they learned that Dr. Peacock's approach was spot-on. Dr. Peacock understood that as these girls starved themselves, the breakdown products of their fat cells would suppress their appetite. If you turned off fat breakdown, they'd become be hungry. With feeding, they began to eat. The thousand calories a day soon moved to fifteen hundred, then to two thousand. Dr. Peacock taught us to go easy with the reintroduction of food, as there were dangers of fast refeeding. Stable and no longer gaunt, just undernourished, the girls were ready for our child psychiatrist to untangle their psyche. The weight gain was the easy part.

There were kid-on-kid injuries. New England children sometimes played a game of "who can sit on the radiator the longest?"—a midwinter sport played when cast-iron boilers flame the hottest. Kids with spina bifida, who had reduced sensation in their legs and bottom, won these contests, sitting on radiators until their flesh burned.

"I was the winner!" yelled a boy with red zebra stripes on his buttocks and legs.

"If I told ya to jump off the Tobin Bridge, would ya do that too?" his mother shouted. Needing skin grafts in stripes where the skin had died, he took his place in the burn center.

Dr. Peacock was also called after a curtain rod sword fight. Two brothers from New Hampshire, eight and ten years old, had taken down a curtain and unshielded the yard-long, quarter-inch round rods, open at one end. They chased each other room to room with arm's-length swings that missed. They then squared off in the living room. Swat one, a miss; swat two, a miss. Lunge one, a miss; lunge two, a miss.

With lunge three, the eight-year-old's sword went into the corner of his brother's eye near his nose. The boy's scream brought the mother home from next door, where she was drinking tea with a neighbor. Not wanting to be caught, the eight-year-old pulled the rod out, yelling at his brother, "Why don't ya stop crying, ya baby!"

The mother came in and saw the rod on the floor, blood and skin at the end. She saw a dime-size red dot near the eye corner of the son sitting blankly on the floor.

There are times when a parent knows what has happened and yet still asks a question with a shake. Grabbing her eight-year-old at the shoulders, she yelled, "What did you do? What did you do? What did you do?"

"Nothing," the boy answered.

Our transport team went to New Hampshire, high-speed transport rights granted, sirens on. Returning, the boy lay quietly in the back of the ambulance heading south on Interstate 93; neurosurgeons awaited his arrival.

"I can't see out of my right eye," the boy said.

"What?" said the transport resident.

"I can't see out of my right eye," the boy said again. The wise resident knew what had happened. She knew the sword had cut the optic nerve connecting the back of the eye to the brain. She then wondered how close the puncture was to the blood vessels at the base of the brain; if they began to leak, it would kill him.

The rod had stopped short of the vessel plexus. However, it had not stopped short of the stalk of the pituitary gland. He would now be a pituitary cripple.

"How will he grow?" his mother asked later when told of the damage. "How will he go through puberty?"

For the rest of the boy's teenage life, Dr. Peacock managed the replacement of the pituitary hormones. He put the boy on growth hormone, thyroid hormone, and cortisone and gave him a synthetic vasopressin, squirted up the nose each night to save water.

At each visit, seeing the boy put on inch after inch, with the confidence every mother needs to hear, Dr. Peacock would say, "Mom, didn't I tell you he'd be fine!"

Abbreviations and Nicknames

Time was precious in our realm—a land of incessant documentation—especially when writing orders and notes day and night, with penmanship varying from poor to atrocious. It was thus not surprising that abbreviations set in everywhere. Some abbreviations were written; some were spoken. Some were medical, some profane.

The medical abbreviations were nearly universal, the same all over town; other abbreviations were our special ones. Simple abbreviations were included in notes:

NAD: no acute distress.

ROS: review of systems.

FU: follow-up.

HEENT: head, eyes, ears, nose, and throat.

History and physical notes used those basic written abbreviations.

Along with abbreviations, we had nicknames, mostly for our notorious patients. "Antonio the Toe" was an entertaining boy from the North End with osteomyelitis of his great toe. He had been stabbed with a pitchfork by his brother, introducing bacteria into the bone that is difficult to eradicate. Antonio the Toe was with us for about eight weeks. He had three operations and remained febrile weeks on end; his bugs were resistant to first-line therapy.

Seeing him bored during his long stay, we invited him to join us in sit-down rounds, where we'd discuss the results of tests and develop plans for that day and the next for the patients in our care.

"Antonio the Toe, what would you do?" the senior resident would ask. And like the medical students on our service, Antonio would say, "I dunno."

Antonio the Toe shared a room with "Jesse the Butt." A football player from Malden, Jesse had been rammed with a helmet in his rear, causing a huge bleed into the gluteus maximus—the muscle named like a Roman general. The bleed was huge. It was drained in the OR and left open to heal. A fist-size divot remained in his right cheek, packed with iodine-soaked gauze.

Jesse the Butt couldn't be on his back and spent his hours rear-end up. To move around the hallways, he was fitted on a stretcher with bicycle wheels so that he could roll himself about. Antonio the Toe, though, would wheel Jesse the Butt in our corridors—Antonio limping with his bandaged toe, Jesse the Butt pointing the direction he wanted Antonio to steer him.

Jesse the Butt was with us for many weeks. Homesick, afraid of the creaks in his hospital room at night, he would park himself at night near the ward secretary's desk, close to the small room where we did our charting. He would sleep where we could see him, snoring on his belly. This might have been a fortunate sixth sense; perhaps he was spying on the nighttime flirting.

One night he was parked before the night secretary, a strong man named Jack. Jack was a good observer with a great sense of humor. Our floors were connected with a pneumatic tube system for sending blood samples from the floor to the laboratory and from the pharmacy to the wards.

We'd tube Jack food. We'd send anonymous "I love you" notes with lipstick kisses on them. We'd tube Jack dirty diapers. Each of these arrivals was greeted by a smile and big laugh.

Jack was forgiving and amused by house officer antics. The clerk upstairs, a married woman in her thirties with Dutch-boy hair, was less forbearing. We listened to her words, delivered in a deep, serious voice, often rebukes of our night moves.

"You didn't really date that Boston College volunteer, did you?"

That night, Jack saw that Jesse the Butt was breathing loudly. Three or four quick breaths, then none for ten seconds, then the quick breaths, then none. This was the pattern of serious illness.

Jack paged us. "Something's wrong with Jesse."

Jesse was 105 degrees and septic. His packing had a foul odor. We wheeled him across the quiet night floors into the treatment room, where the lights were bright, shelves were packed with IV fluids, and stacks of IV catheters were arranged in orderly rows.

An IV was started, the packing was changed, and different antibiotics were given. For the next five days, Jesse was treated in the ICU until his fever passed and he was again well.

Back on the wards, Antonio the Toe was again wheeling Jesse the Butt up and down the hallway. At night Jesse was back in front of Jack, sleeping on his stomach, breathing easily in delighted peace.

Jesse's problems the night he crumped would be charted as:

ROS: rule out sepsis.

AD: acute distress.

Later, in separate charts on the same day, we wrote the best abbreviations of all, "DCTH": discharge to home. Great for them, great for us; these boys were now free to reengage in sport and friends. And as they walked into the elevator, there was a slow good-bye wave from us and Jack, like the wave to a friend you'll never see again.

The resident who had had his car towed by the Worcester cop also had a unique abbreviation set. Whereas the Checkmark Surgeon used to give out quarters in confrontation, the "Acronym Resident" dropped short little bombs with a smile.

SOT.

BFD.

ESAD.

WAH.

He would say these short scrambled phrases and walk away.

"What did he say?" one nurse would ask.

"Not sure," replied the other

"Did he say snot?" another would ask.

"Did he call me snot?

"Did he say why or what?" others inquired,

The Acronym Resident finally had his vocabulary decoded. He felt close kinship with the "Go Fuck Yourself Resident." Knowing that the house officer too needed a polite outlet of distraction, the special code was unmasked.

SOT: suck on this.

BFD: big fucking deal.

WAH: wide ass and hips.

ESAD: eat shit and die.

He continued to recite fifty more acronyms, each acknowledged with a nod from the Go Fuck Yourself Resident.

Knowing of the mishap at the salad bar, the pink shirt at grand rounds, and the guy on the hood of the car, he also introduced PJES: "paroxysmal Johnson exposure syndrome."

Another person with a nickname was "Tags," a sixty-four-year-old man with a transient ischemic attack, the forewarning sign of a stroke. He was cared for by a neurology resident with dark black hair and striking blue eyes that made her look like Wonder Woman.

Cloistered as we all were, she didn't recognize the nickname of one of Boston's "connected"—a member of the North End mob. After discharge, Tags sent her chocolates, bracelets, and earrings. One night he took our group of friends to a North End restaurant where the bill topped two thousand dollars.

Then the phone calls came. "My nephew Tony has a bad back. Can you call in a few Percocets for him?"

She did.

Next his cousin Benny needed pain meds, then Jake and Lisa, then Carl, then Estelle. She was trapped in an insidious web of narcotics prescription. She stopped answering his calls. Strong men with dark hair, shirt buttons open to show off gold chains and hairy chests, began to visit her at work.

"The Tags wants to know if you're all right," one would say.

"He wants you to give him a call," the other would follow.

She was now trapped in a web, gradually spun, from which she couldn't extricate itself. She moved to another apartment, changed her phone number, and went from brunette to blond. The measures were ineffective. Tags's crew stalked her. Finally, following the advice of a detective, she moved to Canada to avoid RIP and DOA.

Some of the abbreviations referred to clinics. NICU-FU stood for "neonatal intensive care unit follow-up clinic." This was where the long-term outcomes of those born too early were tracked. Then there was the HO clinic, the hematology oncology clinic, where kids with cancer received outpatient treatment.

The GLM clinic was the "good-looking mother clinic." Two seniors, strong and handsome, filled their clinics with one gorgeous mother after another. Like a Hollywood pediatric office, there sat blonds and brunettes—thin, clear-skinned, smiling, and well dressed. No other residents were allowed to attend the GLM clinic sessions with them.

We used abbreviations to make rounds move along. Well into our training, we tired of the medical students' presentations of children with gastroenteritis, asthma, and respiratory syncytial virus. Their presentations were exciting for them but pure pain for us as they rattled arcane facts, the consequences of the ridiculous demands that presentations be as complete as possible. They strained to outdo one another in their description of case trivia.

"I found a mole on the instep."

"Someone was mean to this child in third grade."

"They have a Yorkshire terrier that had diarrhea last week."

"This baby is really cute."

"The father smokes."

"The mother is a hooker and got twenty dollars from the father in Room 201 last night."

As the students presented the dull facts that were important only to them, we wiggled in our skin and stared at our watches, realizing that presentation compulsiveness caused them to neglect the heart of the case. Even the Compulsive Senior had reached his limit with the students and formulated a code to be adhered to for presentations.

Using the new code, "1" was mild; "2" was moderate; "3" was severe. RSV referred to respiratory syncytial virus, which clogged the lungs in infants and also infected us each season as colds. AS was asthma, the condition of respiratory tract spasm. ROS was rule out sepsis. NVD was nausea, vomiting, and diarrhea.

Happy to apply these new standards, the students now took the lead in the simplifying rounds. "If this works, can I write it up?" asked one of the students, who helped shepherd her classmates in the new way. Now they would present five patients in two minutes.

"I admitted five children last night.

"Patient 1. ROS, 1. Plan, continue antibiotics and check cultures.

"Patient 2. NVD, 2. Plan, intravenous saline to be followed by clear liquids."

And so it went, the origin of "lightning rounds." The students saw the benefit of this system. There was more time for teaching, more attention for the sick patients too. "The Compulsive Senior is a genius," the rest of us said as he showed that unnecessary detail got in the way of patient care, sucking up time for needed thought.

Lightening our work some, the abbreviations got the better of us too. QD means every day. QID means four times a day. Wags wrote an order for an agent to lower blood sugars QD. With penmanship not the best, the floor clerk mistook the hook of the *Q* for the letter *I*. Thus, the patient received the medication four times a day. Two days later, the elderly man was in hypoglycemic shock, triggering a stroke.

I once wrote an order for the anticonvulsant Phenobarbital for a seizing infant. Instead of forty milligrams, the nurse gave four hundred, my decimal point neither obvious nor circled. Five days later, the infant awakened seizure-free.

These errors happened uncommonly, as the system's checks and balances helped stop these breakdowns, but they did happen. A doctor too tired to form crisp letters and numbers, nurses not experienced enough to know better, and the complexity of those we nurtured with treatment that went beyond the ordinary contributed to these unintended mishaps.

Revealed, these acronyms spread service to service quicker than the news of how our mummy moved. Growing like the *Andromeda Strain*, the acronyms mutated into a new generation of perverse phrases, expanding our under-the-breath dictionary.

And acronym use happened everywhere—the EW, the ORs, the ICUs. And it happened everywhere except in the GLM clinic.

Death, the Proud Brother

We all owe a death, and at Man's Greatest Hospital, for many it came too soon. Just four years post-college and months from medical school graduation, without the life experiences of the Gray Hairs, Wags and I were unprepared for life's early end. When patients died, we asked ourselves what we could have done differently, unless the family of the decedent asked us first.

"How did this happen?"

"He was fine yesterday."

"Tell me exactly what happened," somebody would say among the others grieving. The question meant we were at fault, and requests for records from attorneys would follow.

"How did this happen?" needed an answer. Even though death might have been unexpected, the accumulation of failing hearts, kidneys, livers, and lungs simply meant there wasn't anything left to sustain life.

Death came at all times and in all places. It happened in the ORs; it happened in the driveway circle where the sick were dropped off; it occurred in tiny incubators where infants panted, blue and mottled.

Death came in the morning; it came with lunch. Mostly, death appeared at night. With death imminent, family members would sit by the sick, holding hands—some fat and pulpy, some wrinkled with blue veins shining below transparent skin. Sometimes the hands were tiny, the size of a thumb. But that's not how it usually happened. Death so often happened alone.

"Sure, she'll be okay for a while," we'd say. The family would go to dinner, and then the phone would ring with a cold message.

"He passed away right after you left. I'm sorry for your loss."

The aging and the young died mostly at night. Perhaps they didn't want to scare the living, believing it rude to die with family and friends present. After they died, the decedents were wheeled to the morgue on a special stretcher, empty on top, with white sheets hanging over the bottom where the dead rested. Tubes and IVs were left in place where they had been inserted for the pathologist or coroner to remove. "Mommy, how come no one is on top of that bed?" would be asked as the stretcher was escorted down the hall.

Death came for kids who were infected. Viruses, bacteria, other invasions took them. It came for the kids with cancer. I reflected on Thomas Wolfe's *Death the Proud Brother*—big black horses of death pounding down our wards to take them when their parents were gone. Many of the dead were term and pre-term babies with underdeveloped lungs, with hearts unable to oxygenate their small bodies. At times these were special infants, last hopes after years of fertility problems.

With the sick babies, attachment not well developed; interaction was often a handhold at best. Attachment was there for us with the older kids, whose fate we guided but left in a mental lockbox. Losing these kids, we felt as though we lost one of our own residents. Kids were sometimes desperation coded, but usually morphine or methadone prepared for a dignified death without pain.

When the night stretcher with the white sheets came too often to our floor, the emotions of the ward team began to break down. No fake lab results were printed. No one hacked the laboratory system. No one drew devil horns on photos. The girls wouldn't sleep with their boyfriends, haunted by the faces of the lost.

When the pulse of our group dropped too low, we had "Sidney Freedman Rounds." Sidney Freedman was the *M*A*S*H* television show psychiatrist; short with black curly hair and thick eyebrows, he would appear on the show when the Hawkeye character decompensated.

The role of our Sidney Freedman was played by a child psychiatrist who worked with us and knew our shells and soft spots. We appreciated that mind medicine was as much a part of child care as were drugs and fluids, and we felt lucky to have him as part of our core group.

He'd meet with us as a group or alone if we needed it. As a physician, he knew that death was a sacred, seen, and unspoken part of medicine that circled us. "Cowboy up," he'd say, compelling us to reengage and not mope.

Once, tragedy hit one of my patients. A victim of the poor advice given to me by an EW radiologist, a teen fell dead at my feet. I needed to see Sidney. During our meeting he said, "You either get past this over the next two days or we'll have to look into why you can't."

Sidney Freedman rounds consisted of us talking about the child deaths, our painful feelings of inadequacy, and our fears of call nights alone. Rather that telling us how to cope, Sidney held a mirror that reflected our "whys?" for us to answer.

Seeing each other emotionally naked, we pushed each other out of despair. After each death, we dusted ourselves off and went back to work until the big black horses of death charged down the hallway again to take another young life. Better prepared by the sad cumulative events, we dusted ourselves off quicker and quicker until the next time.

The surgical side of the hospital was different from ours. Death was all around, in part because of the elderly nature of their patients and the trauma and tumors they dealt with. Grandfathers died from incarcerated hernias, from head bleeds caused by calcified arteries, from tumors that migrated from the bowel to the brain. There were highway deaths too that came from flipped cars on Interstate 93 south or T-bones at intersections.

There were also the young deaths on the surgical side. Men and women our age fell to tumors, traumas, and aggressive infections. The surgeons looked at each other, saying, "That could be me. That could be you."

Wags too was involved in a death where, like me, he wished he could have done things differently—the kind of remorse that's agonizing to admit, the kind that keeps you awake when exhausted. He talked to his father, the surgeon. There were no Sidney Freedman Rounds in surgery. A letter to a sad son arrived, brief; his father wrote the surgeon's creed at the end:

This is my scalpel. There are many like it, but this one is mine.

My scalpel is my best friend. It's my life. I must master it as I must master my life.

My scalpel, without me, is useless. Without my scalpel, I'm useless. I must cut with my scalpel true. I must cut better than the disease that is trying to kill others. I must destroy it before it destroys others. I'll . . .

My scalpel and myself know that what counts in this war is not the blood that we shed, the tissue we damage, or the excisions we make. We know that it's the successes that count. We will succeed. . . .

My scalpel is human, even as I, because it's my life. Thus, I'll learn it as a brother. I'll learn its weaknesses, its strength, its parts, its uses, its materials, and its blades. I'll ever guard it against the ravages of weather and damage as I'll ever guard my legs, my arms, my eyes, and my heart against damage. I'll keep my scalpel clean and ready. We will become part of each other. We will . . .

Before God, I swear this creed. My scalpel and myself are the defenders of health.

We are the masters of our diseases. We are the saviors of life.

So be it, until victory is humanity's and there is no disease, but health!

Wags carried this paper in his wallet, worn and shiny. On those blue days, he would take it out and read it, stand, and go back to work. While Wags reflected on the surgeon's creed, I reflected on the words of Thomas Wolfe:

For there is one belief, one faith, that is man's glory, his triumph, his immortality—and that is his belief in life. Man loves life, and, loving life, hates death, and because of this he is great, he is glorious, he is beautiful, and his beauty is everlasting. He lives below the senseless stars and writes his meanings in them.

Each of us, in our own way, learned to take on the face of death. And we each learned to help those new to the hospital night world manage death, the proud brother of the sick we cared for, the proud brother of the young and old when it was their time to move on. And showing no mercy, death came when the dying said "Can I have just one more year, just one more month, just one more day, or just one more handhold."

Road Trips

To begin the academic climb that will reach the MD rung, undergraduates can choose from more than one hundred medical schools in the United States. Only one medical school has a fraternity, and that school is not Harvard, which Wags's father attended.

There were many Harvard legacies—students whose fathers or mothers attended that institution—at Man's Greatest Hospital. Of my group of twelve, six co-interns had gone to Harvard Medical School, several of them legacies. We the non-Harvard wondered if that extra donation to the alumni association, or the donation of a laboratory or building, had moved the applications of the mediocre to the top of the pile. Most of the Harvard grads seemed worthy of the Harvard diploma, but a few weren't. They were less studied, less smart, less hardworking than the rest of us who had clawed our way into the schools we attended.

Some of us went to state schools, not able to afford the huge tuitions of the private schools or not willing to chance mortgage-size debts. Some of us had been accepted to one school, no choice offered.

Some medical schools are labeled "top tier," others "second tier," and others "third tier." These rankings were meaningless when it came to schooling—more reflective of the research done and reputations established over decades. The rankings spoke nothing to how smart the students were, how vigorously they worked, whether the curriculum was soft or not, or whether the graduates were ready to walk the halls of Man's Greatest Hospital. Wags and I found that some of the top-tier legacy graduates weren't up to the level of our supposedly lower-tier schools.

On orientation during my first day at Mass General, I rode an orange elevator that reminded me of a set from the Stanley Kubrick movie *2001: A Space Odyssey* with a Harvard Medical School legacy. New to the area, I asked "What do you do around here?"

The legacy answered. "I mostly sit in my room and smoke pot all day." We carried this fellow's workload over the years that followed.

Another legacy had a father who was a pediatrician. He was neither knowledgeable nor hardworking, and you never wished to share night call with him, as the heavy lifting and decision making would fall at your feet. These legacies were some of the problem children that we policed ourselves; the Gray Hairs stayed out of such messes.

At our schools, thousands of miles apart, unknown to each other, Wags and I had road trips of relief, common in the fact that we never had more than twenty, thirty, or sometimes fifty wrinkled dollars in our wallets. At a time when airfares were cheap, I'd book thirty-nine-dollar weekend flights to Fort Lauderdale with fellow medical students. Five or six of us would fly down on Friday night, crashing at a friend's apartment. After burning on the beach, we returned home Sunday morning. The airline pilots appreciated our routine. At the end of some flights they announced, "Let's hope the medical students make it back to class on Monday." Applause from a jet full of travelers would erupt.

Southern tradition ablaze, Wags traveled with friends to other colleges and medical schools, but by car not jet. His sky-blue Cutlass logged several thousand miles per year on these hauls. Long distances to ride, no time for stopping, he and his classmates wore Texas catheters to avoid bathroom stops. Texas catheters are gross devices hooked to bedridden patients at VA hospitals—condoms with a tube at the end connected to a urine bag that could hold a gallon. Full bags were spilled out of the car windows at eighty miles an hour, dotting the windshields of the cars behind. Some drops blew their way in the open windows of following cars too. As with many of my trips, Wags's trips were visits to college friends, and he too slept on their floors. After the brief visit, the next day they would hit the highway home, filling their bags quicker in a post-drinking-binge diuresis.

All the medical schools in my area had rugby teams, and I played this wild sport, dropping as many kicks as I fielded. One of our classmates had a black funeral hearse that we'd take to matches in Brooklyn,

Philadelphia, and Massachusetts. Twelve of us rode in that with room to spare.

Leaving Brooklyn one Saturday afternoon, rugby drinking games over, my teammate saw a cross street named Rugby Road. The hearse veered up the street and dropped us off two by two to shimmy up street sign poles. We hoped to return with metal namesakes of our sport.

Generally New York City police don't take kindly to out-of-state sign robbers. When three squad cars arrived, we slid down the poles. We explained who we were and frankly admitted what we were up to, explaining that our mission was blocked by sign bolts welded tight.

The patrolmen talked among themselves and then walked over to us. We wondered what the bail would be. The sergeant said, "Young doctors, get outta here. Go home and study." We thanked him for his leniency, hopped back in the hearse, and were preparing for Monday-morning tests two hours later.

After Wags and I arrived in Boston for internship—apartment rooms picked; walls livened with college-style décor; piles of clothes, books, and papers on floors—our Boston road trips began. The Boston road trips were tough to coordinate with our every-other-weekend calls. Most of our trips were our own, save for the one-day rides to North Shore beaches or the Cape.

Others took these trips too. The stories of the weekend past were shared at the Monday-evening meals as we told tales of the New England new to us. We told stories of reverse road trips that happened when distant boyfriends and girlfriends flew in. Usually after a meal and reunion sex, they would watch TV or shop alone while we took our sleep-debt naps. At times it would have been better if that was all that happened on weekends.

One surgical resident, on-call straight Thursday morning through Friday night, was heading down Route 6 lined with green pine trees on the way to the Cape. He fell asleep, crossed over the median, and flipped his car. A *Boston Globe* reporter telephoned the program director. He was told, "No, he wasn't post-call when he was driving. He'd been on vacation all week."

We had the road trips of courtesy too. Those essential trips happened when a former roommate or friend was to marry, as when a college roommate of mine was to be married in New Jersey. My invitation to the girl from Maine to join me was rejected, although she later told me she wished she had come along. "I don't feel comfortable," she said.

I thus called a Cathy, who said, "I would *love* to go."

Down the Massachusetts Turnpike went my white Fiat. Three hours later, we were dancing, laughing, and explaining to the newlyweds, "I just didn't have time to get you that special wedding present you deserve." I knew I had a year for wedding gifts. That year drifted into a decade. Sixteen hours later, back up Interstate 95 north I drove and was on call the morning after I was back in Boston.

I continued to work with Dr. Peacock as the year moved along. After the presentation of the child with the bump, we submitted another abstract to present two children whose blood sugar had dropped, putting them in coma after eating Fruit Loops. "Fruit Loop Hypoglycemia," was the title of the abstract. We worked up the mechanisms. Their stomachs would empty too fast when full of cereal. First their sugar would zoom up and then it would drop, triggering unconsciousness. We were invited to a meeting in New Orleans, where I was to receive special recognition for this work. I received a travel grant—a free room at the New Orleans Hilton on the mouth of the muddy Mississippi. Dr. Peacock heard about this and found me.

"Would you mind if I stayed with you? I couldn't find an open hotel." The obvious meaning was "Why pay for a hotel when I can stay with somebody else for free?"

Down to New Orleans we flew—another two-day break from call granted by my chief residents. On the flight down, Dr. Peacock told how he had clawed his way to the ranks of Man's Greatest Hospital, how a Nobel Prize winner had supported his promotion. He described the inspiration and serendipity of his discoveries, the thoughts behind his success.

He required that I rehearse my presentation three times. "Perfect!" he said. Then it was time for sleep. I learned that night that Dr. Peacock slept in the nude. Perhaps it was a European thing, I thought, since he'd grown up in England.

Three o'clock in the morning, he woke to use the bathroom. He opened the door in the dark room, closing it behind him. He was now standing in the hallway. He took the painting off the wall to preserve some modesty and banged on the room door. Like the night they had painted my toes, I was in one of those sleep-debt slumbers and didn't hear the knock. He paraded his way to a house phone. About ten rings later, I was awakened by a call from the hotel clerk.

The next morning I went for a run to calm my nerves, gratified not to have to dress in the many layers I wore to defend myself against the Boston cold. I came back in an hour; my talk was to go off an hour after that. Showered and dressed, I looked around. "Where are my shoes?" I asked out loud.

I imagined the shame of having to present wearing Nikes. I thought of the shame it would bring to Man's Greatest Hospital. David Letterman could get by wearing sneakers, not I.

Embarrassed, wearing a red tie, a navy blazer, and sneakers, I headed toward the elevator. I stood in front of a long hotel window looking at the muddy river below. Then, like Moses parting the Red Sea, the elevator doors opened and out strode Dr. Peacock.

Standing tall, chest puffed out, he said, "I'm so sorry. I wore your shoes to breakfast by accident." He continued, "They were so comfortable. I went for a long walk. I feel so refreshed."

Shoe swap done, I was up on stage. Questions answered, pulse back down to normal, the road trip was over in several hours. Unlike my talk in Las Vegas, my presentation ranked first! I received a check for three hundred dollars; the runner-up, from the Children's Hospital of Philadelphia, was given fifty dollars for his discovery of Legionnaires' disease bacteria on subway tokens.

Later that evening I was back in the pit. At the evening meal, I told how Dr. Peacock had taken my shoes. I also flashed my prize.

The last road trip of my internship was the most changing. Wags, the Checkmark Surgeon, and I were off to Chatham, on Cape Cod. Four of the nurses on the surgical floor had rented a home for a weeklong vacation. We headed down Route 6, excited for two days off, excited for companionship.

The girls at the house were our age but had been working five years longer. They hadn't followed the long road we had taken, but they knew our path of travail.

Some of the nurses had nicknames. One was "Bubbles" because her cheeks were perfect circles that would pop out when she was in dour moods or brightly smiling. Another was called "Jo," even though her name wasn't anything like it.

One, curvy with beautiful black hair, showed up late wearing a short green sundress. She jumped out of a tan Chevy Impala that she called "Pal," with rusty bumpers and a peeling black vinyl top. Compared to her beauty, this was a mismatch. She bought the car for five hundred dollars because her father liked that it was big and safe, and the ugly car made its trips up and down Route 6 without problems.

While the other girls giggled about their nail color, where they bought their shoes, and how they clogged a feeding tube with peanut butter, she sat waiting to break into meaningful conversation.

It took a while for us to park close to the beach. We soon walked to the ocean's edge, with the Atlantic still early-summer cool. Not knowing one another that well, we sat in our separate groups—the interns and the nurses—telling stories across empty towels. Our towels were the white short bath towels taken from the wards. Theirs were long soft colored towels bought at the better stores in Boston.

Off to an early-season empty restaurant, another of those classic New England buildings with faded cedar-shake sides and a long wraparound porch with white rails, we drank Manhattans into the night. We returned to the beach at night in pairs, not our groups, hoping perhaps for hookups that didn't happen.

Downstairs, our group slept on the floor of a room so dark that you couldn't see your hand touching your nose. Earlier in the week, a family had been hacked to death at a house about a mile away. We feared the same fate in that black night. Perhaps this was why we were invited, decoys for a murder. The next morning we left the Cape early to miss the thick Sunday traffic, as Wags was on call that night.

Back home, Jo, a nurse who left early too, went to the apartment of the Checkmark Surgeon. They fooled around for an hour, then she headed off to her shift, which started at 3:00 p.m. She hadn't wanted her intentions known to the other nurses at the house.

That day and weekend, Wags and I had no such luck. Bubbles made a play for Wags that he turned away because he was after Jo, who was now sleeping with the Checkmark Surgeon.

Two weeks later, I ran into the girl with the decrepit Impala. Walking into the parking garage at night as I was going out, we caught each other's eyes. "That was fun last week," she said

"There's a booze-cruise tomorrow. Want to go?" I asked.

Two harbor cruises, North End dinners, and concerts on the Boston commons later, a good-bye to the Cathys sounded.

My relationship with this girl from Medford, who was as confident as she was beautiful, free of emotional waves, took off, and I felt the first stability of my life. When I cried when the horses of death took my patients and friends, she listened; I no longer needed Sidney Freedman. When attending-versus–house officer relationships decayed beyond reason, she replanted my feet in reality. When she saw that I wasn't recognized for what I had done, she instilled in me the spine that moved me from muttering acronyms under my breath to direct talk.

She recognized that I still needed to grow as much as I needed to learn. She respected my time with Wags, the games at Fenway, my innate selfish compulsion to fill all hours of my days with medicine and discovery.

Now my road trips had a new partner—and my residency a new compass.

Pets of the Hill

The love of medicine is the love of biology, and that love spans a diversity of life. Nurses and doctors thus fancied and acquired a panoply of pets.

With the death of Aristotle, my tuxedo-gray cockatiel with his yellow crests and orange cheeks, who was in the pet cemetery below our apartment window, I stood down in my desire to get another bird. But the cockatiel would resurface.

Leaving the If you lived here you'd be home by now apartment with the girl from Medford, we saw a gray-striped cat the size of a cocker spaniel. It had striking green eyes and sat with cat confidence, soulfully managing an occasional tail twitch. She went over to pet him.

"He's so *cuuute!*" she said petting him, looking up at me, delighting in a new friend. She missed that he was now vomiting; the perceived purrs were the regular jerks of retching.

She looked down. "That's gross. It's your bird!"

Interspersed in the spewed meat loaf were tiny gray feathers that could have belonged to any of the local sparrows or pigeons. Yet also mixed in was the yellow crest of the cockatiel. There were mouse tails and small toes too. Like the raiders who first stole our mummy, the feline had found our mouse pit.

"Serves him right," she said. The cat walked ten feet to the right, where he vomited more of Aristotle.

Dr. Bigelow was also a fancier of fowl. With a large red barn behind his house, he stocked it with Rhode Island Red chickens and Sebright bantam roosters. He had geese and complained about how greasy their eggs were when scrambled.

He had a special fondness for the Sebright bantam, a bird without a wattle—a testosterone-responsive flap of skin that grows red and beefy in other roosters. The roosters' feathers looked like those of the hen, not bright as in other breeds.

The Rhode Island Red roosters humiliated the Sebright bantams, stealing their food, taking their nesting material, pushing them aside when the wood bucket of fresh water arrived in early morning.

The Rhode Island Reds teased the Sebright bantams as well.

"How inadequate do you feel? Look how small your wattle is. And you can get hens with that little thing!

"Har, har, har!" the Rhode Island Reds rooster would say before going off to mount a hen.

The Sebright bantams, though, knew their stature at Man's Greatest Hospital. It was the Sebrights that led to the finding of hormone resistance, a great discovery. This bird, not the one from the tiny state, paved the way to recognition of pseudohypoparathyroidism and pseudopseudohypoparathyroidism, putting Man's Greatest Hospital's physicians on the Mount Everest peak of endocrinology.

Dr. Bigelow's barn was full of feathered fowl that nested on rafters, in hay-stuffed eaves, in cracked old snow tires on the barn floor. At first light, they would announce the start of the day, to the neighbors' disdain.

When the neighbors expressed their displeasure, Dr. Bigelow would answer, "I think they were here well before we were," justifying the birds' place in Boston's suburbs.

One day I traveled to Dr. Bigelow's house for dinner with Dr. Yogur. We looked at the barn and birds and then had a great meal. When it was time to go, Dr. Yogur's Mustang wouldn't start. Opening the hood, we saw that the carburetor was clogged with dust, dirt, and feathers. He sprayed some ether on the carburetor and turned the ignition. But the motor didn't start, and the engine erupted in fire. Dr. Bigelow was relieved; a gas leak was the problem, not the rooster feathers.

Dr. Bigelow drove us back to Boston, with Dr. Yogur reminded in a nauseated flashback of the days when he drove with Dr. Bigelow to conferences in Providence.

Other attendings liked dogs, more specifically, English bulldogs. These were the attendings that came up to Harvard from Yale, where the squashed-nose breed is worshiped. A Harvard football coach still remains cursed to this day at Yale for strangling a bulldog before a Yale-Harvard football game to inspire his brainy athletes.

Dr. Seagull, who had owned generations of bulldogs, cared for children with kidney diseases. Some diseases presented at birth, others happened after children were infected by eating *E. coli*–contaminated hamburgers or drinking unpasteurized apple cider at state fairs.

I can't imagine a less-affectionate or less-desirable pet than a bulldog, which spends most of its life poorly oxygenated because of its squashed airways, a consequence of trait selection gone awry. When Dr. Seagull traveled, he would ask me to house-sit to feed his bulldog, Tiger. A "plasticovore," the dog ate TV remote controls, the plastic case where Dr. Seagull stored his reading glasses, large plastic mixing bowls, and full and empty Coke bottles. Dr. Seagull's life revolved around dog defense, the protection of all things plastic against a breed with no short- or long-term memory.

Memory blank, the eighty-pound stout, piebald, brown-and-white dog could jump four feet—the distance from the ground to a bull's snout, I imagined. After his jumps, he would stand on the granite kitchen counter moving one leg slowly before the others skated out from under him. This would be followed by a thud. With no memory of previous counter-top falls, his greatest conquest came when he ate two dozen freshly boiled eggs, shells too, four at a time from a colander in the sink.

He made his way onto the kitchen table too. Pot roast meals disappeared in the time it took to get biscuits from the oven. Tiger needed discipline, so Dr. Seagull called "Bud the Dog Trainer," whom he had hired two years earlier to instill manners in Tiger when it was a toddler. Bud accepted the invitation for dinner. The doctor's wife was a marvelous cook, and pot roast was served to elicit the dog's worst behavior.

As the dog moved to the table, Bud stood, saying a stuttering "N, n, n, *no!*" Tiger rolled over like a sinking boat, four legs up and still. You could have stuck journals between his legs and left them there until the next issues arrived, he was so still.

Dr. Seagull was amazed at Bud's power, his training secrets hidden, as sessions with the dogs were executed in garages without owners. Muffled shouts of "N, N, N, and No!" could be heard from driveways. Dr. Seagull imagined his dog suspended from a choke collar learning to associate "N, N, N, No!" with strangulation.

During dinner, Bud said, "I, duh, duh, don't see a problem. La, la, like Nancy Reagan says in her a, an, antidrug ads, ja, ja, just say no!"

As soon as Bud backed his car out of the driveway, the dog was back on the table, eating the family's dessert and the plastic spoons too.

Another time, I was house-sitting on a weekend off from call when the phone rang. "Hello," I answered.

"Eh, eh, it's—"

"Bud?" I answered.

"Yeh, yeh, yes."

He explained that he was making a Christmas card with his favorite and best-looking obedience school graduates. He wanted Tiger—for his looks, not his brains, he joked.

The grouping would be the dogs of Boston's rich and famous. To complete a bulldog trifecta, he had a French bulldog owned by Arthur Fiedler, the conductor of the Boston Pops, and an American bulldog that belonged to a Red Sox outfielder. A pair of hyperactive Jack Russell terriers—one rough-coated, the other smooth-coated—belonged to a singer in Aerosmith, he said. A white fluffy Samoyed, owned by the king of the Boston mob, was included, "or else."

Peering into his small Volkswagen Golf, I observed that the bigger dogs were in the back, with the Jack Russell terriers in the front passenger seat. Each dog looked straight ahead, not barking, not jumping. The English bulldog sat between the two terriers in the front seat as Bud drove to the photo shoot. A photo was delivered two weeks later to the doctor's home. The dogs were sitting in front of a Yale-blue background, attentive like third-grade elementary school children posed for a classroom photo.

On the back of the card was a small note: "Thanks and happy holidays! Can you believe this was the first shot!"

Dogs were all over Boston for their owners to enjoy, but many were pests. As we ran on paths along the Charles, the dogs walked by young women were our nemeses, genetically programmed or trained to keep males away. They would bark, snap, and sometimes bite us.

Some of the women of the Charles walked their dogs off-leash. As I was running one day, a black Labrador-shepherd mix took up chase, snapping two feet behind my heels as I ran two miles to the Harvard boathouse. When I was far enough away from his owner, it stopped. I felt bad for this girl, whose nice morning walk had turned into an unplanned two-mile run.

Dog crap was everywhere in Boston too. During the summer, it desiccated on hot days. In winter it froze. Like sunflower seed shells scattered in a baseball dugout, the dog droppings littered the sides of the paths along the Charles in mounds, waiting for the spring rain to make them disappear.

While running in summer, we saw a baton-twirling guy on in-line skates. Thin and well muscled, he would sail up and down the macadam paths shirtless, a whistle in his mouth to signal pedestrians. He would twirl his batons in front of curious canines, hitting them on their snouts and making them scamper back to their owners.

In winter I would see the surgeon who was the basis of the character in John Irving's *The Fourth Hand*. He ran with a lacrosse stick, flipping dog turds onto the frozen Charles and cursing the young dog walkers.

Another attending raised goats, which he used to generate antibodies for his research. He would inject these animals, which had weird keyhole-like yellow eyes, with serum. Two months later, he took four ounces of blood, saving only the clear part. This part had the special antibodies he was developing.

One Saturday he found that the goat inoculated with the serum of the boy with the pillowy cheeks was walking with a wide gait, its belly swollen. He had read that goats get "bloat," which causes their hay-digesting stomachs to swell. *This could be fatal,* he thought, and decided to drop a tube into the goat's stomach and decompress the rumen.

He explained to Nikki in the EW that he needed three Ewald tubes and left with them tucked under his coat. At home he summoned his son—six feet, two inches tall; tan and thin—who worked in his father's lab during high school summers. His other son was completing a tour of punk rock concerts along the East Coast and wasn't there to assist.

The father and son straddled the goat, the son holding the horns, the father trying to pass the tube through the mouth. They found that goats are even less cooperative than strong-willed cardiac surgeons.

"I'll hold his mouth open—you pass the tube," he said to his son.

Chomp. The tube was three inches shorter.

"Try again!"

Chomp. The tube was again shorter.

After three tubes had been chewed into sausage-size pieces, they tried passing a tube through the nose. Unlike my luck with Miss New York, ruining her nose job, the tube wouldn't pass; the goat remained bloated.

In medicine we say, "If you can't get at it from above, you go from below." Two enemas flowed into the goat's rectum, the white stumpy tail boinging up when the nozzle went in.

The next day, the goat's yellow eyes were swollen shut, puffy like uncooked pizza dough. The ears were fat and pulpy like the loafers worn at Mass General. The rectum looked like a cauliflower.

Failure admitted, the attending visited a local veterinarian, a rare trip for MDs who routinely administer people medicine to animals. No mention was made to the vet of the Ewald tubes or the enemas.

"When did you last see the goat urinate?" the vet asked.

"I'm not sure," answered the doctor.

"Your goat is in kidney failure," she explained. "If you castrate goats too young, the phallus won't grow and they're prone to urinary tract stones. They need a special diet with ammonium chloride to keep this from happening."

The MD said, "I have that chemical in my laboratory. Do you want me to go get some?"

"*No!*" answered the vet.

With his son's assistance, he helped the veterinarian try to catheterize the goat. Goat anatomy isn't like human. The penis is retracted, hidden in a goatskin sheath. They tugged with clamps and pushed tiny catheters without any luck.

"How valuable is your goat?" asked the vet.

"*Very*," the MD said.

"We have two choices. One, we euthanize the goat. Two, we send it to the Vet School at Tufts, where they can perform a diverting ureterostomy, letting the kidneys drain from the animal's side. It costs eighteen hundred dollars."

The veterinarian called for a pet ambulance to transport the goat. She suspected that the MD would contact his urology buddies to perform the procedure at no cost. After all, many medical staff pets had been treated in OR3. A week later, after being operated on at the veterinary school, the goat's enema-induced edema was gone; the eyes opened, and the goat resumed chewing hay.

Everything happens for a purpose. Now the goat had side-draining ureters, making it easy to collect the urine the attending would test for antibodies. He brought a gallon to work.

"Eureka!" he yelled the next week. The antibodies were in the urine; no more bleeding would be needed. He saved the goat's urine by the gallons. With enough available, he could now isolate the mysterious protein hormone from the child with the pillowy cheeks.

One year later, in the journal *Science*, he reported a new variant of adrenocorticotropic hormone, ACTH. Normally the hormone is only made by the pituitary. This boy with lung disease was making it in his pulmonary cells.

For his discovery he was recognized by the National Academy of Sciences. In humility, he named the hormone for the child. When he was on stage receiving the award for his discovery, he wondered if the goat would supplant the Sebright bantam rooster as the greatest pet of Man's Greatest Hospital.

Discoverers and Discoveries

"Discoveries went out from Man's Greatest Hospital, but discoveries never went in," they still say.

The basement of the brick building, four floors below the pediatric wards, housed the laboratory of a Nobel Prize winner. In a methodical, nonflashy manner, he unraveled the metabolic workings of cells, the Krebs cycle, a pathway known to wise biology students. These were the footsteps the Gray Hairs wanted us to follow—in wildly unrealistic expectation, Wags and I thought.

Recognized for a discovery when he was a young man, he tinkered quietly, unassumingly, dissecting the metabolic pathways that cause cells to tick. As the years marched on, just a few grasped his discovery. There was an occasional point made as we passed by. "He won the Nobel Prize." Medical students would say "Really?" and continue their paces.

Man's Greatest Hospital was the place where ether was first used in surgery, or so it was claimed. One hundred and fifty years earlier, black-clad physicians in white aprons laced with bloody streaks had hacked a jaw tumor off a man. Ether had been patted on a small white mask over the patient's face, a mask that looked like a miniature badminton racket.

As good as the surgeons were, their success often rested in the hands of the anesthesiologists. With the new era of anesthesia, the prominence of the institution rose with each inhaled breath of the acrid gas. The best surgeons flocked to Man's Greatest Hospital to ply their trade. More and more increasingly complex operations followed.

There were also the "Salt and Water Boys," as Dr. Bigelow dubbed them, speaking with longing fondness. Conscientious objectors in World War II, they defined water balance as we know it. First these boys were deprived of water to define "the floor," or how little water we could live on. Then they were flooded with gallons of water to define "the ceiling," when water intoxication set in. We learned of these studies and the contributions these volunteers had given to the pilots flying over the Pacific. Shot down, floating in life rafts, they now had defined amounts of water to drink each day to stay alive.

One day the Salt and Water Boys had a reunion at Man's Greatest Hospital. They walked in tall and trim, gray haired, a half century past their courageous youth. We gazed at them with the same admiration given the Nobel Prize winner.

At conferences and during grand rounds, presentations of science, of discoveries that wouldn't help us now but might in a decade or two, were presented. Posters of upcoming talks filled the bulletin boards. There were more postings for talks than for cars for sale or apartments for rent. The journals we read were about science and discovery too. There was also the surgeons' journal, we joked—*Sports Illustrated*.

These layers of science immersed us in a land of discovery. We learned that the science of medicine wasn't the chin-on-the-hand images of gray-haired investigators in white coats. Residency applicants wrote and talked about wanting to enter research, interest that we scanned for in interviews. The research road was long, requiring a mind-set different from that of the pre-med and medical students.

Our medical school success rested on memorizing the facts we'd pack in our minds. We created mnemonics to memorize cellular pathways, not knowing their functions. These were the skills from which *A*'s on tests sprang, not the skill of creativity that led to discovery.

When asked to engage in research, we found it tough. Clinical medicine always presented a lead to follow.

"Where did the fever come from?" Do X, Y, or Z.

"Why do the lungs sound wet?" Get a chest X-ray.

"Why is the patient urinating so much?" Get a urine culture and check for diabetes.

"Why is the neck stiff?" Do a lumbar puncture.

For discovery, I would learn that solo moments of reflection are needed, time when minds are free of lab results, free of phone numbers to call for X-rays and scan results. The required silent time was so different from our resident pace, where we shuffled through index cards of lab results and charged down hallways in response to code calls.

When our second year of residency hit, we were comfortable with the sick, the simple, and the serious. We became comfortable with family's tough requests and their nuttiness. We could comprehend and deal with death. And just when patient care became natural, we were pushed to leave our comfortable ward settings for laboratories to become discoverers.

Straddled in the middle of the five years of surgical residency was a mandatory one- or two-year stint for research. Within pediatrics or internal medicine, the three-year clinical stint wasn't interrupted by more than two months; the years of research would follow later for the interested.

One of our colleagues went to England to work on coronary blood vessels in mice. Under magnification, he sewed tiny vascular grafts that were of the size of human hairs. Another of our colleagues, who was in college by the time he was fourteen years old and graduated medical school when he was twenty, went to learn lung transplant biology. The transplants he did in pigs were a prelude for the work he did in adults.

Wags picked up work in a crosstown laboratory, probing pancreas inflammation. The person he worked with was stiff and unemotional, always thinking, always serious. For his time in the lab, Wags wrote three papers as the lead author. He too experienced the pride and nervousness of national meeting presentations. But his time with the research bench wouldn't continue after the year in the lab passed. Back to the EW, back to the wards, and back to the ORs he went—his comfort zone.

His discoveries came later, when he modified the nips and tucks of the generation of surgeons who came before him. He discovered a new approach for pancreas removal, a procedure he conceived while operating on white mice. Now young trainees worldwide say, "I'll use the Wagner modification of the Whipple procedure."

But Wags didn't make his discovery at Mass General. He created his fame in an operating room in St. Cloud, Maine, where he assumed the practice of hospital alumnus Dr. Wilbur Larch.

While I was on a road trip in Mexico with the girl from Medford, Wags was home alone for a week. He ambled to Faneuil Hall for dinners alone on his off-call nights, comfortable to sit in the same booth at the same restaurant three nights running. The same waitress took his order each night. She was a pretty girl with short brown hair and a black skirt above the knee like a Boston regular. Yet her accent was different from the Boston natives; she spoke with the long drawn-out syllables of Maine. After the third dinner, they recognized each other to mutual blushes and laughs.

"Did ya evah pay your friend baack?" she smiled.

"No waaay!" he said with a laugh.

"How come you're working here?" he asked.

"I got laid off and didn't want to go back home." She answered.

"Wanna go to a Sox game?" he asked.

After a long pause, she said, Cathy style, "I'd *love* to."

I imagined that Wags's next road trip was to Maine in the summer, where he cursed the icy water but marveled at the dynamic blue skies and jagged coast. As he took in Maine's jagged coast while finishing his third lobster at a restaurant on the water, she remembered him drinking from a carafe of wine. Perhaps she was also thinking of his special talent, revealed above the Boston skyline the year before.

During my residency, I dabbled at research only a little, not having much time. My years of research training would come when I was taken under the wing of a wild-haired scientist from Nebraska who had trained at Mass General a decade earlier and then gone to the National Institutes of Health to become a scientist. Falling into science, he persevered, not caving into the comfort of the otoscope or the prescription pad that he would never pick up again.

"Focus and think," was his motto. "Everyone is smart here. Everyone works hard here. You have to work even harder and longer than they do if you're to survive."

The Nebraskan taught me to unwind from my clinical frenzy, teaching me how to focus on clear, elegantly simple questions. He taught me how to think from different perspectives. He taught me the compulsiveness of hangdog science. He showed me that the comfortable but mediocre projects that some of my peers pursued would be career-stoppers, pushing me to projects of future direction.

When I generated bad data, he said it was time for me to cut my losses and move on to something new. "As my grandpappy used to say, you can't polish a turd," he would say with a laugh. And after Dr. Bigelow and Dr. Ren left this earth and Dr. Peacock and Dr. Yogur moved away, he stepped into their shoes as my confidant and friend.

My start as a discoverer didn't come easy. More in tune with the constant motion of the wards and EW, the sit-down lectures of Dr. Yogur, and the reflex response to the patients before me, I was not capable of dealing with idle time to think. I confessed to Dr. Bigelow and to Dr. Peacock my insecurities and struggles in the lab. They each pushed me to persevere, keeping tabs on my progress and anxiety from a squint-eyed distance.

"You need to calm down and to stick with it," Dr. Peacock implored. "Think back to how tough your first IV was after you walked through the doors here. Was that easy?"

Such were the lessons these men had learned when they were younger. Such were the admonitions they had received from their mentors, who flipped on office light switches Saturday and Sunday mornings, even when slowed by unkind age. Dr. Bigelow and Peacock knew the way whereby Man's Greatest Hospital made discoveries go out by growing the discoverers within.

As time went on, I understood their paternal intentions. Following the course they pointed, I stuck with the scientist from Nebraska. I learned how to design experiments, how to draft grant proposals. I learned the disappointment of failed experiments. I learned to enjoy precious successes, to be savored for just a moment until the next finding came. I learned that you're only as good as your last publication and that your ego rose and sank with grant success, like how our spirits waxed and waned with our patients' fates.

Standing in the shadow and reflection of those who came before, my time would one day come when, as a professor at an Ivy League institution, it was my turn to flip on the light switches on Saturdays and Sundays. Even without gray hair, I was now a Gray Hair, cracking the complex cases as my mentors had done for me. It was my turn to make discoveries novel and important. It was my turn to groom the trainees—both the obvious problem children and those who flew just below the radar. It was my turn to look for those students with the flash of brilliance to send to Mass General to launch splendid careers.

And with every toggle, I reflected on those who guided me. I reflected on those who were now among the senseless stars and the others still writing meaning in them. I reflected too about how I wanted to see these men again to ask just one more question—not about a patient, not about a rare case, not about an experiment. I wanted to ask them, "Did I accomplish what you expected of me?"

I want to ask them the question framed in Man's Greatest Hospital's lobby the years before: "Was I still the runner-up resident?"

The Pendulum Stops

Like the gentle arc of a clock's pendulum, swinging with perfect regularity until the swinging and the chimes that announce time suddenly stop, the days of our early training counted down.

Interviews and selections over, a new group of interns flew into town looking for apartments that would be their base—where they'd recover from night call and sleep debt, where they would soon ponder the difficult cases, where they'd plan and navigate a way to learn.

They would soon learn of Fenway Park, the Cape, and the bars in town—the essence of sanity in an insane world of disease. Their long days and nights of training would stack on top of one another, eventually giving them needed confidence to care for precious lives and futures.

They would find there was no one time, neither after a tragic code nor after a case of meningitis cared for, that would make them step back and say, "Now, I'm a doctor." Our training never done, humbled by our perpetual inadequacy, we were made doctors only by the salutations of those who addressed us as such.

We charged through our days and nights ambitious and boundless, but over the times that followed, some of us became sullen, bored by the tedium of office management, billing forms, and insurance company dealings necessary to keep income steady. Some took jobs in the Midwest. Prospering in cities where they say "This is a nice place to raise kids," all the while longing for the splendid days of swimming in the New England Atlantic and drinking cold beer while cheering at Fenway Park.

Those with ambition in research started programs of discovery, many of which blossomed and prospered. Others started careers with great momentum, only to lose funding just as they were flourishing. Stethoscopes were again worn to earn a living.

Some joined the ranks of Yale, the Mayo Clinic, Johns Hopkins, and Harvard, climbing the academic ladder. Some made discoveries that would change medicine.

Some were taken by death. We watched our friends die of cancer, HIV, overdoses, and crashes.

No matter how our careers unfolded, our reflected memories remain the same. We all think of the Gypsies in the lobby and those who wandered off the street to join us during our evening meals of grand stories.

We remember the nighttime antics in the ORs, the EW hoaxes, the codes on the wards, the trips up and down Interstate 93 to bring back the sick, and the trips of relief to the Cape.

We think of those who took us under their wings, pushed us, demanded of us—making us better physicians and people than we ever dreamed we could be.

We look back with the pride of knowing where we walked.

We look back to when we were young, learning, muttering our own vocabulary, biting our lips as we struggled to cope with the vile things that infected our days and nights.

We smile in homage to the infirm and recovered, our patients and our mentors, the alive and the dead, our indelible friends of peer and faculty—those who shaped us.

We look to those majestic days and smile inwardly, thinking of where we once were and where we are now.

We reflect on our time at Man's Greatest Hospital, when none of us walked with feet of clay.

END

Acknowledgments

Special thanks to Carol, Danielle, Jeff, Mike, Mark, Terry, and Melreen, who helped shape this book. I am grateful to my editor, Tom McCarthy, whose encouragement and keen eye got this to the finish line. Many thanks go to Julie Castiglia for her representation.